9

Terrorism, Protest and Power

Terrorism, Protest and Power

Edited by

Martin Warner
University of Warwick

Roger Crisp
University College, Oxford

Edward Elgar

Published by
Edward Elgar Publishing Company Limited
Gower House
Croft Road
Aldershot
Hants GU11 3HR
England

Edward Elgar Publishing Company
Old Post Road
Brookfield
Vermont O5036
USA

British Library Cataloguing in Publication Data

Terrorism, protest and power.
1. Political movements
I. Warner, Martin *1940–* II. Crisp, Roger *1961–*
320

ISBN 1 85278 202 1

Printed in Great Britain by
Billing & Sons Ltd, Worcester

Contents

Contents

PART III POWER

Foreword

The essays that follow have been prepared under the auspices of the Society for Applied Philosophy. Those by Harry Beran and David George were directly commissioned for this volume. The contributions by Robert Phillips and Anthony Quinton were originally presented to the Society's round table on Terrorism and Violence at the World Congress of Philosophy in August 1988. Versions of all the remaining papers were prepared for its May 1989 annual conference on Protest and Power; in accordance with normal practice the Conference Address by Paul Gilbert will also appear in a forthcoming issue of the Society's *Journal of Applied Philosophy.* We are grateful to members and associates of the Society participating in these events for their comments and criticisms, many of which have been taken into account in the final drafting, and to those who contributed other discussions from which we have learnt but which were not appropriate for inclusion here.

Notes on the Contributors

Harry Beran is Senior Lecturer in Philosophy at the University of Wollongong. He is the author of *The Consent Theory of Political Obligation*.

Martin Bull is Lecturer in Politics and Contemporary History at the University of Salford. His research and publication focus is in the field of Italian politics.

Stephen Clark is Professor of Philosophy at the University of Liverpool. He is the author of *Aristotle's Man, The Nature of the Beast, Civil Peace and Sacred Order* and various articles in libertarian and communitarian political philosophy.

Roger Crisp is British Academy Postdoctoral Research Fellow and Honorary Junior Research Fellow at University College, Oxford, and a member of the Executive Committee of the Society for Applied Philosophy. He has published articles in various areas of philosophy.

David George is Lecturer in Politics at the University of Newcastle upon Tyne. He has recently published articles on terrorism in academic journals and is currently writing a book on terrorism and related forms of political violence.

Paul Gilbert is Head of the Department of Philosophy at the University of Hull; his main research interests include the philosophy of personal and social relations.

David Gosling is Senior Lecturer in Philosophy at Staffordshire Polytechnic, where he teaches social and political philosophy, the history of ideas and contemporary epistemology. In addition to his research into the ethics of political protest, he is also working on obligations to the Third World and ethical issues raised by the AIDS crisis.

Heta Häyry is Lecturer in Practical Philosophy and Matti Häyry Junior Research Fellow at the University of Helsinki. In Finnish, they have co-authored and co-edited several books on moral and social philosophy. In English, their publications include articles on applied ethical issues in many academic journals.

Susan Mendus is Lecturer in Philosophy at the University of York, where she was Morrell Research Fellow in Toleration between 1985 and 1988. She is Hon. Secretary of the Society for Applied Philosophy. She is the author of *Toleration and the Limits of Liberalism*, and her main areas of research are political philosophy, and philosophy and feminism.

Robert Phillips is Director of the Program for War and Ethics at the University of Connecticut. He is the author of *War and Justice* and numerous articles on ethics and international affairs. He is foreign policy consultant to WFSB television, a member of the Advisory Board of the US Global Strategy Council, and has served as a consultant on terrorism to various governmental and private groups.

Anthony Quinton (The Lord Quinton, FBA) is Chairman of the British Library, President of the Society for Applied Philosophy and a member of the Council of the Royal Institute of Philosophy; he was formerly President of Trinity College, Oxford. Among his books are *Utilitarian Ethics*, *The Politics of Imperfection* and (as editor) *Political Philosophy*.

Richard Tur is Benn Law Fellow at Oriel College, Oxford, and Hon. Treasurer of the Society for Applied Philosophy.

Martin Warner is Lecturer in Philosophy at the University of Warwick and a member of both the Executive Committee of the Society for Applied Philosophy and the Council of the Royal Institute of Philosophy. He is the author of *Philosophical Finesse: Studies in the Art of Rational Persuasion* and of a number of contributions to the study of rhetoric, ethics and applied philosophy.

Paul Wilkinson is Professor in International Relations at the University of St Andrews' and Director of the Research Institute for the Study of Terrorism and Conflict. He has written extensively on terrorism, from his pioneering *Political Terrorism* to his recent revised edition of *Terrorism and the Liberal State*.

Introduction

Martin Warner and Roger Crisp

I

If each of us could have whatever we wanted, we might well run into problems similar to those faced by King Midas; but those problems would not be political. Conflict between the desires of different individuals is a necessary condition of politics. Given that human beings are not angels, it follows that certain people will be left unsatisfied by political decisions; they may also be dissatisfied with the very way those decisions have been made.

Sometimes, individuals are prepared to accept compensation for their desires not being fulfilled through the political process. If the Department of Transport decides to build a motorway through the site where your house now stands, you are unlikely to be overjoyed. But if you are offered a reasonable alternative house, and some financial inducement to move, you are also unlikely to feel cheated. Here, at the level of what we might call *personal wants*, trade-offs are common, required and acceptable.

You might have other desires, however, which would not properly be characterized as 'personal' . These might be desires that whales not be killed, that further attempts be made legislatively to prevent racism in employment practices, that blasphemy against Islam be outlawed, that full democracy come to South Africa, or that the Six Counties of Northern Ireland remain within the sphere of jurisdiction of the United Kingdom. Such desires (accompanied as they characteristically are by beliefs that the satisfaction of the desire is right) we may characterize as being governed by *political* (or *politico-religious*) *ideals*. Here trade-offs are not so common, and often would not be acceptable. A useful indicator of the type of considerations at issue in a given conflict of desires is the perceived relevance of the most widespread medium of exchange – money. No amount of money donated by the Icelandic government is likely to assuage the concern of an adherent of Greenpeace that whales continue to be slaughtered, and arguments based on the comparative prosperity of South Africa or the United Kingdom relative to other African states or to the

Republic of Ireland are characteristically dismissed by the ANC and Sinn Fein as irrelevant. Whether one believes that trade-offs are required even in cases such as these will depend on one's views of the status and methods of politics.

These essays in applied philosophy concern that area of political decision-making in which political ideals are included as variables. When members of a liberal democratic state dissent from the practice of the state, or from the practice of a certain group of individuals within the state which the latter sanctions through its inaction, they have a number of options available. They may write to their MPs, Congressmen or similar representatives, or to the press, or they may join or initiate a lobby group to campaign for reform. They may, however, avoid these channels, or find them unproductive. Instead, they may attempt to express their discontent through disobeying a statute or ordinance, in order to draw to public attention either the injustice of the law in question, or injustice elsewhere in the fabric of the state. An alternative to civil disobedience is revolutionary or subrevolutionary terrorism. This is perhaps the most extreme form of dissent short of all-out civil war; indeed there are some who see terrorists as engaged in war. These means of dissent are not, of course, mutually exclusive.

At its most radical dissent may involve denial of one's membership, in any but the most formal sense, of the state in which one is physically set – either because it holds territory to which one believes it has no right, or because it is itself illegitimate, or both; the standards of legitimacy are characteristically set here by one's political ideals. When such a dispute involves disagreement about the appropriate source of legitimation the conflict may be more than usually intractable, for the standard democratic procedure of majority vote by the legitimating 'people' (*vox populi, vox Dei*) is fatally flawed when the question at issue is who 'the people' are. The more intractable the dispute the more likely, other things being equal, that dissent will take illegal or terroristic forms. But even in less radical cases, one's conception of the nature and normative limits of the state is directly relevant to issues concerning the justifiability of illegal expressions of dissent. For politics is essentially involved in the resolution of conflict, in our era primarily by the organs of the state, and it is often these organs – or the ways in which they are put into operation – to which those who engage in terrorism or civil disobedience are objecting. No discussion of the legitimacy of protest can properly be conducted without reference to that of the structures or practices to which objection is made; power is but the other side of protest.

II

Terrorism

'One man's terrorist', so the cliché goes, 'is another man's freedom fighter'. The relativistic attitude implicit in this statement has practical consequences for states within which it is widely shared, inhibiting certain types of counterterrorist strategy, but it also encapsulates a conceptual thesis. The relevance of philosophical analysis to political life is here at its most obvious – disagreement (often unrecognized) about the nature of terrorism runs deep and wide, and muddled thinking in this context is liable to lead to confused action.

On the face of it, as David George points out, the cliché is absurd, for it runs together two completely different types of definition – one by reference to means (terror), the other by reference to ends (freedom); further, there is no necessary connection between the two, for terror may be used for ends other than freedom and freedom may be fought for by nonterroristic means. To this one might object, with George, that 'terrorism' is not (or not merely) to be defined in terms of terror, and that more subtle criteria are required for distinguishing terrorists from freedom fighters.

This is the type of approach favoured by the report on Social Order presented to the 1988 Lambeth Conference. Maintaining that 'it is vital to distinguish between acts of terrorism and the legitimate struggle for liberation' it presents a set of 'searching questions' in order to enable us to 'decide which description is the most accurate' in any particular case, questions which are strongly reminiscent of the classic requirements for a Just War (Lambeth 1988: 177–80). Not surprisingly, while the Conference supported certain types of civil disobedience and 'understood' those choosing 'the way of armed struggle as the only way to justice', it made no sympathetic reference to terrorism as such; 'terrorism', on the account provided by the report, is by definition illegitimate. This reflects an essential evaluative element in those popular conceptions of terrorism lying behind the cliché; to designate an act as 'terroristic' is to condemn it, whereas to associate it with 'freedom' is to commend it. When this evaluative account is coupled with relativistic assumptions about value itself – which of course was not the case at Lambeth where the relevant standard was taken to be 'the mind of Christ' – the disabling relativity of the cliché appears inescapable.

For legal purposes such an approach is clearly unsatisfactory; thus the current legal definition of 'terrorism' in the United Kingdom eschews evaluation and prefers an instrumentalist account, referring to both means and ends and including mention if not of the legally problematic 'terror' at least of 'fear':

> 'terrorism' means the use of violence for political ends, and includes any use of violence for the purpose of putting the public or any section of the public in fear.
> (Prevention of Terrorism (Temporary Provisions) Act 1984, s. 14(1))

There are obvious problems with this definition, for as it stands it classifies as 'terrorism' such diverse phenomena as riots, revolutions and robbing banks to support the Party, none of which are normally so characterized – thereby blurring otherwise clear, and arguably morally significant, distinctions. Further, warfare is a paradigmatic use of violence for political ends, yet few governments regard warfare as essentially terroristic; given the context, one is tempted to read the definition as implicitly reading 'the *illegal* use of violence for political ends' but, quite apart from the hint of circularity this involves, such a definition would exclude most forms of 'repressive' or 'state' terrorism, whether that of the French Revolution sanctioned by 'revolutionary legality' (for which the word was coined), of Stalin (as instanced by Anthony Quinton), or of the government of China after the 1989 events in Tiananmen Square.

Nevertheless the definition goes some way towards incorporating a number of descriptive features of the everyday concept of terrorism which the more evaluative conceptions tend to marginalize; both Anthony Quinton and Paul Wilkinson set out in their essays to explore versions of this concept, the former arguing not that it is 'above criticism, only that it is familiar, unitary and internally coherent', testing paradigmatic varieties of terrorism against common linguistic intuitions and acknowledging the existence of borderline cases. There is a familiar problem here, that of reconciling the plurality of instances of a kind with the unity that makes them so classifiable. The ancients referred to it as the problem of the One and the Many, and the Socratic attempt to find unitary formulas to encapsulate the necessary and sufficient conditions for the application of important practical concepts is today viewed with disfavour; but the Socratic practice – better than the underlying theory – of attending to specific instances and exploring their interconnections and differences is excellently adapted to the attempt to understand the phenomena in question, and it is on this enterprise that Quinton is engaged. Such understanding is important if we are to enquire generally, as Wilkinson is concerned to do, into the political, moral, historical and sociological status of terrorism, without having to restrict the scope of our enquiry to a particular terrorist campaign or group, or even a particular act. Further, how terrorism is to be responded to, from both practical and jurisprudential points of view, is a question best answered on the basis of an understanding of the phenomenon itself.

But where disagreements run as deep as they do here, this type of approach has its limitations; Quinton does not claim that the concept he articulates is ' above criticism' and, as we have seen, rival concepts are also current which are more evaluative than instrumental. Although there have been periods when the term ' terrorist' was characteristically worn as a badge of honour, today, as Wilkinson notes, the term tends to be rejected by those to whom it is applied. It is this feature of contemporary usage which is presupposed in the Lambeth report and one that needs to be related to the more descriptive features presupposed by the lawyers and explored by Quinton. The instrumentalist definition employed by the Prevention of Terrorism Act facilitates the assimilation of terrorism to crime, whereas the criteria proposed at Lambeth point rather to the analogy with warfare – where the criteria are not met the warfare is unjust and terroristic, but in other cases it counts as legitimate struggle. Neither concept of terrorism is above criticism, and behind them lie rival models of human community. This is the theme of Paul Gilbert' s essay; as so often, intractable conflicts at the practical level are symptoms of less obvious clashes of political ideals – but these latter are not beyond the reach of rational discussion either. Gilbert argues that the more defensible of such models cut both ways; they may be able to ground claims to legitimacy by certain types of state, but may also justify some terroristic campaigns.

Further, the structure of reasoning used by those who defend actions that on the instrumentalist account are terroristic – exemplifying the deliberate pursuit of public, social or political ends by the use of terror, or at least by means to which physical violence is essential – has its own characteristic features, with distinctive credentials which need to be assessed. Robert Phillips instances the ideal of popular sovereignty, the principle of self-determination, and ethical consequentialism (the doctrine that consequences determine moral value) as historically lying at the root of much contemporary terrorism as displayed in its characteristic justifications; examinations of the latter demand a critical scrutiny of these more abstract considerations. His own examination leads to a certain scepticism about the underlying concepts, together with a more negative assessment of terrorist campaigns than that of Gilbert.

But negative assessments are also possible with a lesser degree of scepticism about such presuppositions. The most purely philosophical of these is ethical consequentialism; Quinton rejects blaming the widespread adoption of this doctrine for the current prevalence of revolutionary and subrevolutionary terrorism on the ground that it is not uncritical about either means or ends. Both these and other forms of terrorism may well be in part a product of ethical consequentialism, but if as such a terrorist I am to justify what I am doing in consequentialist terms, there are certain hurdles I must leap, many of which are likely to be sidestepped in practice.

I must first compute the expected benefits of my course of action. If Phillips is right, and no large-scale campaign of terrorism against a modern state which has even a shred of popular support has succeeded, these may well amount to almost nothing. Second, I must put in the balance the costs – considering not only the harm I shall bring about locally to the specific victims of my act; terrorism produces anxiety and insecurity at a global level, and this harm is not negligible. Third, I have to consider whether the costs and the benefits are commensurable at all (bearing in mind the difficulty of trade-offs between political ideals) and, if they are commensurable, whether the benefits outweigh the costs. Finally – and this is something often ignored in consequentialist calculations – I must, as Quinton concludes, consider whether there are better alternatives to the option I am contemplating. If Wilkinson is right in his claim that in every case in the past quarter century where democratic rights have been gained and dictatorship undermined, this betterment has been achieved by means other than terrorism, such considerations may have a significant ethical bearing on my decision, in the name of 'freedom', to embark on terroristic activity – which characteristically involves the maiming and killing of people who are to all intents and purposes unconnected with the state of affairs to which I am objecting.

III

Protest

Civil disobedience is an alternative means of expressing dissent or bringing about political change. It is generally less violent than terrorism, and more aptly described as a form of protest. Characteristically, too, it is concerned to bring attention to a specific wrong which is believed to exist rather than to undermine the authority of the government. Sometimes civil disobedience will be employed to protest at a practice which also has a terrorist campaign directed against it.

As in the case of terrorism, there is a preliminary question – Socrates' 'what is it?' – concerned with characterizing civil disobedience. It is primarily this issue which concerns David Gosling. On the basis of the position adopted by John Rawls, Gosling attempts to pin down the nature of civil disobedience before moving on to discuss consequential questions. Rawls's thesis is an appropriate touchstone for such a discussion, for there is a close link between the notion of civil disobedience and liberal political theory, while Rawls's *A Theory of Justice* is widely regarded as the most important book in the liberal tradition since John Stuart Mill's *On Liberty*.

The link is most easily grasped historically. As the medieval world view began to change from the fifteenth century onwards, political philosophers began to experience a sense of insecurity – expressed in its most intense form, perhaps, in the writings of Thomas Hobbes. A form of individualism developed in which a human being's position in the cosmos – and in particular that part of it constituted by the state – was not to be explained and justified in a top-down way. Rather, the existence of the state had to be justified by reference to its members. This was the origin of social contract theories of political obligation, and the problem faced by Hobbes, Locke and Rousseau was that the existence of such a contract was hard to demonstrate. The legitimacy of disobedience to the state had been seriously considered as early as Plato's *Crito*, but it now became a pressing issue; social contract theorists assumed that individuals had a natural right to disobey and that therefore the state with its demands could be justified to its members only by showing that this right had been waived and hence no longer existed, at least in its original form. This final qualification is important. If the waiving of the right is construed as resulting from a contract, it becomes relevant that a contract is binding on all parties concerned; if one party defaults or acts in ways that contravene or exceed its terms this may affect the obligations of the others concerned. Thus it was widely acknowledged that the right to disobey could be circumscribed without its disappearing altogether.

Of course contemporary liberal theory does not invoke the myth of a social contract in its pure Lockean form, but it nevertheless is concerned to show that a contractual element is implicit in the relation between individual and state; Rawls's model of the 'original position' plays a role analogous to that of Locke's myth. Given such a conception of political obligation, in certain circumstances disobedience to the demands made upon individuals by the state may well be justified: if, for example, that demand was itself unjust, or if disobeying it might play a role in a morally legitimate protest against other demands of the state – perhaps on other of its citizens. Such assumptions lie behind Gosling's essay. Just as it is important for governments to be clear about the nature and moral bounds of terrorism, so it should be a matter of concern for individual citizens in a liberal democratic state who retain some allegiance to democracy to determine the limits of political obligation in the face of perceived injustice; here political theory can become part of political practice.

Reciprocally, it is desirable for governments of such states to be sensitive to the proper limits of authority implicit in the structures and practices on which they depend and that legitimate them. David Gosling considers the implications for the individual when a state appears not to be thus responsive, but for the essays by Heta and Matti Häyry and Susan Mendus it is the nature of those limits themselves which is under scrutiny. In the modern world liberal democratic societies are typically pluralist, in the sense that significant numbers of citizens hold differing and competing political ideals; this raises in an acute form the problem, adumbrated earlier, of the extent to which a government may legitimately adjudicate or require trade-offs between them. The way one resolves it will affect one's answer to the question: Should the state be prepared to accept civil disobedience as morally justifiable if it is based on the lack of consensus concerning those basic values that lie at the heart of political ideals? The claim that it should was recently argued in the context of a report on nuclear power in Finland, and it is to that claim that the Häyrys' paper constitutes a reply. On analysis the claim appears radically problematic, for either it licenses a permissiveness towards lawbreaking that is liable to undermine the authority of any government of a pluralist society (what is sauce for the nuclear protester's goose is sauce for the antiabortionist's gander), or else it points the way to a form of value despotism that is incompatible with liberal democracy. Indeed, the thesis that democratic decision-making can only work properly where a value consensus prevails rests upon a remarkably pessimistic view of the possibility of resolving political conflict through such procedures. In a liberal democracy, to resort to disobedience without first seeking such resolution of differences, on the ground that there can be no trade-offs between political ideals, might be thought to be somewhat presumptuous.

Some, indeed, would go further. In his *Democracy and Disobedience* (1973) Peter Singer argues that those who think they must disobey democratic laws in order to avoid acquiescing, or seeming to acquiesce, in particular results of the democratic system are mistaken: their actions are really indicative of a refusal to acquiesce in the democratic system itself. (Singer 1973: 104)

But in avoiding Scylla we are here in danger of being sucked down by Charybdis. If the Finnish report sets the limits of state authority so narrowly as to be incoherent, Singer is in danger of eliminating them altogether in a manner reminiscent of the more extreme advocates of untrammelled Parliamentary sovereignty. While the Häyrys are concerned to criticize an argument designed to narrow those limits, Susan Mendus seeks to show that they nevertheless exist – and that hence when they are overstepped civil disobedience is permissible even in a democracy.

In elaborating his version of the social contract Locke introduced his famous notion of tacit consent; although few of us explicitly undertake to abide by the requirements of the institutions of the state within which we live, in making use of the laws of the land we nevertheless give tacit, implicit, consent to them. Analogously, Mendus introduces the notion of tacit dissent; one may dissent from a belief by refusing to affirm it when required to do so, and justify this silence as part of the right to freedom of speech. This form of silence she relates both to that claimed as part of the right of an individual to avoid self-incrimination and to that telltale kind which suggests that a view is not being given a fair hearing. Contemporary liberal discussions of the first two forms of silence depend on a double dichotomy between opinion and information and between self-development and the public interest which is itself deeply flawed. Where matters of opinion are at stake, it is widely held, the right to free speech – including the right to silence – may be defended in terms of the desirability of safeguarding the development of the individual personality; but where this is not the case the public's interest in the disclosure of information needs also to be taken into consideration. In such terms it is difficult to defend the right against self-incrimination, protected in Britain by common law privilege and in the United States by the Fifth Amendment, as anything other than a 'guilty man's privilege'; whereas the individual may properly have priority in matters of opinion, the public interest, it would appear, takes precedence where facts are concerned. It is hardly surprising that this right is currently under attack.

But Locke's classic defence of toleration makes no use of the concepts involved in the double dichotomy. For him there are supremely important religious truths which are not mere matters of opinion, but this does not

license – to use Queen Elizabeth I's expression – making windows into
men's souls; rather, the proper considerations relate to the rationality of
persecution and the legitimate aspirations of civil authorities. The question
of how far the state can be tolerant or intolerant is prior to that of how
tolerant it should be – 'ought' implies 'can' – thus the irrational aspiration
to achieve the impossible cannot be legitimate. Light is needed to change
men's opinions, but light cannot be attained via the coercive means at the
disposal of the state, so these means are in principle inadequate to achieve
authentic religious conformity. Mendus argues that these considerations
can be extended to the rights to free speech and against self-incrimination;
any attempt to enforce the handing over of conscience to the state beyond
certain limits is irrational and hence oversteps the bounds of its own
authority, thereby legitimating civil disobedience. It is the requirements
and intrinsic capacities of statehood itself that set bounds to the legitimate
aspirations of Leviathan.

IV

Power

We have seen that models of terrorism and civil disobedience are closely
related to conceptions of the community and the state. Terrorists are
usually and civil disobedients almost always members of states, in the
sense that they have a nationality and are legally subject to one or a specific
number of governments. Often it is to the existence, characteristics or
actions of states that they object, with their actions aimed directly against
state institutions and officials. Given these links, some consideration of the
nature and normative limits of the state is clearly appropriate. However,
whereas we have seen reason to hold that questions about the nature of
terrorism and civil disobedience are prior to those about justification, it can
be argued that this may not be so in the case of the state. We have a rough
grasp of the notion, prior to analysis, and if we can show that all the main
institutional structures which give form to it are unjustifiable, then more
delicate characterizations may be superfluous. State power may be the
other side of terroristic and civil disobedient protest, but perhaps the coin
itself is illegitimate.

What, then, might be a good reason for the existence of the state? One
such might rest on the analysis of politics suggested at the outset of this
Introduction: the state exists to resolve conflict. Now one question we

might be tempted to ask of the Leviathan when faced with a high incidence of terrorism is whether it is doing what it is supposed to do. If not, then one option would be to replace the present state mechanisms with updated models. Another would be to ask the deeper question of whether we could not resolve conflict without relying on the existence of a state.

Let us assume, for the moment, that we could do without the state. The next question an anarchist will have to face is how we are to advance towards utter statelessness. Many have thought that anarchism points to terroristic, violent and revolutionary means of change, but Stephen Clark argues that this need not be so. Anarchists believe that means determine ends, and thus social change which is initiated on 'archist' assumptions might well be thought undesirable. By analogy with Just War Theory, Clark contends, a theory of the 'Just Revolution' emerges from anarchist presuppositions, a thesis with obvious implications for the viability of anarchist terrorism. Further, since there are techniques for social transformation other than that of revolution, and given that means determine ends, some analogues of civil disobedience may also have a role to play in anarchist thought.

Perhaps the only kind of state which is likely to be accepted by an anarchist will be a Rousseauian direct democracy, in which there is unanimity on every issue. The only reason for the existence of a state like this would be to solve cooperation and coordination problems; coercion would be no part of its remit. But this of course is an unattainable – and by no means universally attractive – ideal, despite the fact that certain states in certain times and places have come closer to it than others. In practice desires conflict, rendering necessary the exercise of power which will inevitably be unequally distributed – thereby raising the problem of conceptualizing this distribution: how, for example, are we to understand the position of those groups in a position of weakness vis-à-vis groups which are politically dominant? Here, once again, the Social Order report to the Lambeth Conference is useful:

Power may be described as the capacity to make and enforce decisions. . . . In social and political terms it is to be in control of and to manage the institutions that affect the lives of others. This includes the transmission and perpetuation of the binding myths and traditions of culture. Those in power are the keepers of the symbols of authority. To have power is to be at the centre of the decision-making process. (Lambeth 1988: 168)

The exploration of power in terms of centre and periphery is the concern of Martin Bull, using as a case study the southern question in Italy. Here we find Bull using procedures we have noted elsewhere, assessing the coherence and cogency of various models of the phenomenon concerned, and again the importance of clarity in definition and assumption is stressed: which of the models is to be preferred is likely to depend on one's conception of the status of peripheral power groups in the first place. On one plausible account the relation between centre and periphery is to be defined in terms of the location which embodies the value system by which a society is ordered; but given this model the Italian example points to the disconcerting consequence that a periphery may modify a centre, a conclusion not without its relevance to those protesters, discussed by both Gilbert and Gosling, who feel their values, myths and cultural traditions to be marginalized by those at the centre of the decision-making process.

Sometimes, however, the time-scale required for such modifications is taken to be unacceptable and certain groups, normally peripheral though sometimes in the political ascendant, express a corporate wish for an existence separate from the state of which they might be considered a part. This may be seen as a breaking away from, or as a denial of ever having been a constituent of, the state concerned. But, as we have seen, the problem of assessing such aspirations is bedevilled by disagreement about what counts as a legitimating group. Robert Phillips, Harry Beran and Richard Tur all point to the claim expressed in the Universal Declaration of Human Rights that 'All peoples have the right to self-determination', as also to its problems. For Phillips the principle is very nearly void for uncertainty. The dispute about whether the inhabitants of the Six Counties rather than of Ireland as a whole count as a 'people' in the relevant sense underlies the current campaigns in Northern Ireland; as Phillips remarks: 'terrorists continue to fly the banner of self-determination'. Thus Harry Beran is concerned to examine the fundamental but remarkably unexplored issue, occupying a position that straddles national and international law: Who should be entitled to vote in self-determination referenda?

Beran's strategy is to explore the implications of the right to self-determination in the light of those principles which the liberal democracies have propagated and which underlie the primary documents of contemporary international law. From the perspective of liberal democracy the unity of a legitimate state must be voluntary; thus self-determination is the right of every group which has awareness of itself as a distinct group, is territorially concentrated and is viable as an independent political community. Expression should be given to such principles by the reiterated use of the majority principle – a procedure which is capable of giving the required content to the notion of a 'people' – taking account of an appropriate set of criteria, which Beran is concerned to develop and apply. Gilbert suggests that this approach may be required when the individualistic Hobbesian conception of the state is wedded to the theory of popular sovereignty expressed through majority rule; but other models of human society may ascribe importance to communities with claims on and obligations to those who would secede from them, and in such a perspective the principle of self-determination as clarified by Beran may no longer be regarded as overriding. If this is so, such considerations may indicate certain limitations in classic liberal democratic theory. Once again, seemingly intractable political disputes reflect less obvious clashes of political ideals.

To return to Hobbes, it is sometimes argued that we should see states, which are sovereign in their own territory, as analogous – at the international level – to individuals in the state of nature. There is no superstate, though there are, of course, coalitions of states which can apply sanctions either to recalcitrant fellow members or to states outside the coalition, and this fact bears upon Richard Tur's concluding discussion of self-determination and sovereignty. From the perspective of international law states are not quite like Hobbesian individuals, in that they enter contractual arrangements with prior commitments to moral and political principles by which they see themselves as bound; nevertheless there are important analogies, not least the way that contracts can transform the moral world. Both considerations bear on pressing practical issues; for example the doctrine of the Just War invoked by other contributors presupposes that in some circumstances warfare is a legitimate option – and such circumstances may be identified by reference either to illegality (breach of contract) or to those prior principles and ideals.

The undertaking of war against states which act unlawfully is not an option which is always employed, nor is its outcome certain; since international law includes the principle of effectiveness (the international community deals with the successors of Lenin, not of the Tsar), it may on occasion be rational for a government that regards current arrangements as unacceptable to undertake international lawbreaking with the aim of altering the incidence of legal rights and duties. Such lawbreaking, Tur argues, may be assimilated to civil disobedience – albeit on a large scale – exemplifying the legal principle *ex injuria ius oritur*. At both the national and the international levels there are times when lawbreaking may be a means of law making or changing, and it may plausibly be argued that any rules defining the legitimacy of governments are defeasible. If such considerations are not merely to act as a fig-leaf for 'Might is Right' they need to be governed by certain criteria; as within states, so between them, too permissive an approach to civil disobedience is self-defeating. The analogies between the two spheres are instructive. Somewhat as Plato maintained that our understanding of justice in the human soul may be sharpened by seeing it writ large in the laws of a well ordered state, so our grasp of justice in the state may be improved by examining the principles governing relations between states. Ultimately all serious discussion of terrorism and civil disobedience, at both the national and the international level, has to tackle the question of the legitimacy and proper interpretation of that ancient legal principle cited above: Under what conditions may justice proceed from injustice?

Prologue

1. Community and Civil Strife

Paul Gilbert

I

Writing of the state of nature in which there is a 'warre of every man against every man' Thomas Hobbes noted that

> it may peradventure be thought, there was never such a time, nor condition of warre as this: and I believe it was never generally so, over all the world: but there are many places, where they live so now. For the savage people in many places of *America*, except the government of small Families, the concord whereof dependeth on naturall lust, have no government at all; and live at this day in that brutish manner, as I said before. Howsoever, it may be perceived what manner of life there would be, where there were no common Power to feare; by the manner of life, which men that hath formerly lived under a peace-full government, use to degenerate into, in a civill Warre. (Hobbes 1962: pt 1, ch. 13)

Hobbes may have known something of civil war, but he was wrong about Red Indians. The Iroquois and other woodland tribes of whom he must have been thinking had a formidable reputation for savagery in what one anthropologist describes as a 'war of nerves whose weapons were torture, ambush, ruthless massacre and even the howl in the night' (Farb 1971: 106). But these wars, although often between Iroquois speakers, were external, not civil, conflicts, depending on the internal unity of the tribes. Their lack of coercive government, which shocked Hobbes, later excited Engels (1884: ch. III; quoted in Farb 1971: 100): 'no soldiers, no gendarmes or police, no nobles, kings, regents, prefects, or judges, no prisons, no law suits ... all are equal and free – the women included' he enthused. Engels's picture of a natural community of equals was wrong as well, though his reference to women was significant. Concord among the Iroquois, while wider than that which 'dependeth on naturall lust', was apparently maintained through a rigidly stratified matriarchy.

Hobbes and Engels exemplify two views concerning the character of a community. For Hobbes a group can live a common life only if governed

17

by rules which are imposed upon individuals by threat of force. For Engels a common life is possible, in principle, without coercive rules, although at particular stages in history such government may be required to hold individuals together under rules. For the Hobbesian, therefore, civil strife presages the disintegration of the community itself, since the coercive force of government is no longer able to compel obedience to rules. For the anti-Hobbesian the effects of civil strife depend upon the strength of communal relations without the coercive force of government.

It is, I suspect, an *a priori* Hobbesian fear, rather than an empirically informed anxiety, that strikes many of us when we are confronted with civil strife. 'The main point about terrorism', says Robert Phillips (1984: 89) for example is this:

> every political community has understood that random and indiscriminate vio-
> lence is the ultimate threat to social cohesion, and thus every political commu-
> nity has some form of prohibition against it. Terrorism allowed full sway would
> reduce civil society to the state of nature where there is in Hobbes' fine
> description, 'continual fear of violent death, and the life of man, poor, nasty,
> brutish, and short'. No political society can sanction terrorism, for that would
> be a self-contradiction, as the very reasons for entering civil society were to
> escape precisely those conditions imposed by the terrorist

Political theorists are confident, however, of securing empirical evidence to support this Hobbesian thesis. The only way to convince its opponent, suggests J.D. Mabbott (1947: 21–2), is to invite him to 'live in a country where authority has disappeared ... if the country is in a state not of "battle" but of "war"' – he means "civil war" – 'he will soon discover the meaning and prescience of Hobbes' gloomy imaginings. I lived', he reports, 'for a month in Ireland in 1922. There was no actual loss of life near us during that time, only a few shots audible in the night. Yet there were fear and suspicion everywhere and all peaceful avocations had come to an end. Fear and veiled hostility had destroyed the whole structure of social life.'

It is such apprehensions that lead to talk of waging a 'war against terrorism' on behalf of society itself, a strange 'war' that can sometimes justify internment of this implacable enemy's sympathizers but refuse prisoner-of-war status to its soldiery, a war which curtails society's freedoms in order to defend a free society.[1] Is this war against terrorism warranted by a threat to social cohesion? To answer this question we need to become clearer as to what terrorism is, and what kind of threat it might pose to a community.

II

There are, I think, two paradigmatic approaches to characterizing terrorism. Though many current accounts combine elements of both, it is worth isolating them since each depends for its immediate plausibility, I believe, on fundamentally different conceptions of community.

The first approach I shall consider regards terrorism as a form of warfare, in which fear is spread by attacks upon noncombatants contrary to the rules of war. This view, which we may refer to as the Unjust War model, attempts to characterize terrorism in terms of notions taken from the theory of the Just War. Just War Theory holds that the intentional killing of the innocent is a violation of the principle of discrimination required for *jus in bello*. The innocent include most members of the civilian population, who should not be harmed because they play no part in perpetrating any wrongs which might provide one side with *jus ad bellum*. Terrorism, it is held, offends against this principle. Its aim of inducing capitulation through fear is achieved by direct attacks on civilians, who are in no way involved in producing the injustices complained of. This is not just a tactic of terrorists, but an essential feature of terrorism itself.

It is fairly clear that this account needs further refinement. It is surely going too far to suggest (Teichman 1986: 96) that 'terrorism essentially means any method of war which consists in intentionally attacking those who ought not to be attacked'. Many breaches of the rules of war which prohibit attacks on noncombatants do not count as terrorism. It may be that aircraft pilots who bomb population centres are as morally blameworthy as car bombers can be, but if they are the legitimate agents of a state that is waging open war they do not count as terrorists. The same would have to hold true if they were agents of a revolutionary force in an open civil war. To distinguish terrorism from other warlike attacks on ordinary citizens the Unjust War view needs to add that terrorism is a secret or clandestine war, as against an open or declared resort to force. Such a distinction though necessary is by no means clear, but its true significance will emerge later.

One thing wrong with the Unjust War model is surely that the agents of the state as well as ordinary civilians can be *victims* of terrorism. Terrorism as generally understood is taken to include attacks on policemen and security forces, at least so long as they are not engaged in offensive military operations. Many terrorist campaigns, like the IRA's, ostensibly restrict themselves to such targets. It cannot be objected that policemen and soldiers are really noncombatants after all, just because the state claims that they are only engaged in law enforcement. If the terrorists *are* engaged in war then there must be some distinction among possible targets between combatants and noncombatants. War implies combat and hence cannot be waged purely by attacks on noncombatants. It is no doubt to preserve their view of terrorism as a method of war that Just War theorists (see Teichman 1986: 67, 95; Coady 1985: 62) seem prepared to classify policemen and security forces as combatants. They therefore wrongly deny that attacks on them can commonly be terrorist.

The view that terrorism must be an attack on noncombatants springs from the conviction that terrorism is wrong. But what is wrong with attacking noncombatants? Is it wrong because they are, as Just War theory describes them, innocent? Here we need to make a crucial distinction, not observed by Just War theory, between those who are obstacles to one's goal and those who are opponents of it. If one believes one has a just cause, then one will not regard one's opponents as innocent. But the point of one's campaign is to rectify the injustice they may have helped to perpetrate. If one's opponents are not in themselves obstacles to that – they are standing unarmed in the government building which one needs to secure, for example – then one has no need to mount an attack on them. By contrast obstacles to one's goal – the conscripts guarding the government building, say – may need to be attacked, even when they are sympathetic to one's cause. The justification for the prohibition on attacking noncombatants in wartime is that they are not obstacles to military goals, just as soldiers who have laid down their arms are not. If terrorism is war then terrorists must be able to launch attacks on obstacles to their goal of forcibly dismantling and replacing the government machinery in a certain territory, and these obstacles may include people who would in other circumstances count as noncombatants. They may also include not only soldiers but the politicians who control them.

According to the Unjust War model terrorists really are waging war. Yet in practice governments are seldom prepared to concede that they are, preferring to treat them as common criminals, denied the protection that combatants enjoy in war. That governments react to it in this way seems to me a necessary feature of terrorism, unnoticed by the Unjust War model. The kind of factional warfare which the Unjust War model of terrorism depicts simply does not yet count as terrorism even if it involves outrages against civilians. It is not just that terrorism is a modern concept, but that terrorism is a modern phenomenon made possible by the prerogative of the modern state to treat an internal attack on its forces as a crime, in just the same way as an attack on its civilian population.

It is treating terrorism as a crime which turns it into secret war. Terrorism, I suggested earlier, is not a feature of open war. It is sometimes thought to be so through confusing crimes against the rules of war with crimes against domestic law. But it is precisely because terrorism is refused the status of war, so that the rules of war are not applied to it, that terrorism is not open war. And the refusal of the status of war springs from treating all terrorist acts – be they against civilians or soldiers – as breaches of domestic criminal law.[2]

III

In the light of this it is not surprising that contrasting with the view of terrorism as Unjust War stands a view of it as a species of Political Crime. As an example of this sort of view, consider a recent characterization of terrorism as

> the resort to violence for political ends by unauthorised, non-governmental actors in breach of accepted codes of behaviour regarding the expression of dissatisfaction with, or dissent from or opposition to the pursuit of political goals by the legitimate government authorities of the state whom they regard as unresponsive to the needs of certain groups of people. (Lodge 1981: 5)

Such characterizations, more common among political theorists than philosophers, identify terrorist acts as breaches of the criminal law, rather than of the rules of war. These breaches are committed for political ends which ought to be pursued in accordance with the procedures permitted under a legitimate governmental authority. What makes terrorism wrong on this view is not only that it involves violence against citizens, but also that it bypasses constitutional procedures and thereby threatens the legitimate authority responsible for protecting citizens.

The Political Crime model of terrorism can allow that sometimes resort to violence for political ends may be justified. This might be the case if there were no adequate channels for expressing dissent or if the government was not legitimate. In these cases, it may be suggested, violence against politicians and those implicated in the running of the state could be justified. But we should not confuse the Political Crime model, as I characterized it, with the quite different view, advanced for example by Michael Walzer (1973: 199–200), that terrorism is politically motivated crime directed at ordinary citizens rather than against politicians and the like. The Political Crime model proscribes as terrorism even violence against politicians if the political system is open and legitimate, for in that case politicians are simply representatives of the people.

Here, however, is an affinity between these two views of terrorism as political murder. In both there is emphasis on the *innocence* of its victims: in Walzer's, because ordinary citizens must be innocent while politicians may well not be; in the Political Crime view, because politicians following 'the accepted codes' of a legitimate political system are, like ordinary citizens, innocent, while those not doing so may not be. This emphasis naturally contrasts with the stress on noncombatant status in the Unjust War view. What it brings into focus is the political motivation of the terrorist. The right course for a group with political grievances is to bring pressure to bear on those who oppose their aspirations. Only if there is no legitimate authority or proper procedure for dealing with grievances could violence be justified, and then only if it was directed at the politicians responsible for the alleged injustice.

The Political Crime model of terrorism appears to carry with it a chilling consequence for ordinary citizens. Since it is the citizens as a whole, rather than groups of politicians, who possess sovereignty in a democratic state, it is ordinary citizens who would seem to be the natural targets of terrorist groups which have a grievance against the state. The Political Crime view of terrorism can offer no special reason for not targeting ordinary citizens, unless the associated democratic theory can show that violent opposition to the will of the majority could never be justified. Indeed, this is what theorists like Paul Wilkinson (1977: 40) assert: ' it can never be right for minorities', he claims, ' to use violence to try to coerce the majority or the government into submitting to their demands'. But this optimistically assumes that a majority can never act unjustly towards a minority in a way that democratic channels cannot correct. The recent treatment of Catholics by the Protestant majority in the North of Ireland seems to constitute a counter-example. Would Protestant civilians at least then be justifiable targets of terrorism? It is only because terrorists characteristically deny the legitimacy of the state that they escape such a conclusion. If they deny the state's legitimacy they cannot normally hold its members indifferently responsible for injustice. They will pin responsibility on those members who are able to benefit from an illegitimate state by perpetrating injustice in its name. But if the state's illegitimacy gives terrorists a reason for war, they have, as yet, no reason for attacking such people. For, as we have seen, it is not political opponents, but obstacles to victory, who are rationally targeted in war.

Modern states, for reasons which we shall soon investigate further, are predisposed to identify themselves with their citizens. They therefore put their citizens in fear whenever they are challenged by terrorism, for citizens are brought to see themselves as potential victims of political retaliation. The only way for a state to allay this fear would be to recognize that terrorists are waging war. Then it could insist that the rules of war forbidding attacks on ordinary citizens should be observed and take precautions to prevent them becoming the unintended victims of military operations. Instead modern states prefer to regard these attacks as political crimes and are therefore prevented from adopting the different outlook of Just War Theory to them. In this respect modern states curiously collude in spreading the fear which terrorists intend. They would have no option if the Political Crime view were evidently correct. Yet it is open to criticism.

What the Political Crime model fails to do is to specify sufficiently clearly the kind of political motive required for antistate terrorism. Not just any kind of political violence counts as terrorism. Characteristically, I suggest, it is the kind that is designed to overthrow the state or dismantle government in some of its territory. Revolutionaries who overthrow the state by terror but then go on the rampage cease to be terrorists, even if they continue to have political motives, for example to draw attention to the plight of landless labourers. The political motive required for antistate terrorism is precisely the kind of motive required for war – to deprive a government of control over some or all of its territory, usually because the state's legitimacy there is under challenge. The Unjust War view has a clearer sight of the characteristically warlike aims of terrorists, and, if suitably clarified, of the nature of their proper targets. It fails to relate those warlike aims to a challenge to a state's claim to exercise legitimate authority over a territory. The Political Crime view, by contrast, sees that ostensibly legitimate authority is under threat from terrorists. It fails to allow that if that is the terrorists' aim, then, assuming that the state resists and that the terrorists use sufficient force in pursuit of their objectives, they are committed to engaging in war.

The reason why this conclusion is resisted is, of course, that it seems to call into question the characterization of terrorism as a kind of crime. If terrorists are waging war surely they should not be treated as criminals. Yet on the Political Crime view there seems every reason to treat them in this way. As so often in philosophy, each of the views mirrors in its advantages the drawbacks of the other. In order to account for this situation I shall turn to discuss the conceptions of community associated with the two models.

In doing so I hope to shed some light on how the community is affected by and might reasonably react to terrorism.

IV

Given the origins of Just War Theory it is unsurprising that the conception of community associated with the Unjust War model of terrorism is in origin a medieval one. The community is regarded as a group living a common life in accordance with its own rules, but which normally needs a ruler to enforce them. The possibility of a common life in accordance with rules, however, does not derive from the presence of the ruler. On this Communitarian conception, wars are struggles between potential rulers for the control of the territory that supports communities, and internal conflicts are not in principle different from external ones. Now it is evident that the concern of the community is to emerge from war as unscathed as possible. And why should it suffer? For it is rulers, not the communities they rule, who are the parties to the war.[3] A similar view also has attractions for a Marxist. If states are class states why should the working classes, which lack power, suffer in conflicts between different sections of the bourgeoisie? There is, of course, a difference. For the Marxist, the breakdown of law enforcement by the state in civil strife may be a positive good, providing the opportunity for the development of working class institutions to take its place. To the medieval mind it is scarcely that. The important point is that for neither does civil strife automatically threaten the existence of the community. It follows that the community need have no special commitment to upholding the existing state. The community is in debt to the state which enforces community rules but that debt could be outweighed by other factors. That is why the community need have no reason to regard the state's security forces as entitled to the same protection from attack as it claims for its ordinary members. In particular it can regard civilians as entitled to the protection of the law against direct attack, but not the forces of the state whose proper remedy lies in military countermeasures. There is on this conception no necessary sense of the state belonging to the people who make up the community. This conception offers no account then of the relations between the community and the state that can show why internal attacks upon the forces of the state should be regarded by the community as crime. This feature of the Unjust War model of terrorism derives directly from its associated conception of community.

The Political Crime model of terrorism evinces the contrasting Hobbe-

sian conception of community with which we started. In this it is better
tailored to the conditions of the modern state than its rival. It recognizes
that the maintenance of order in the state is accomplished by the impartial
application of its laws even to those seeking to take power by violence,
rather than by resort to military force against its rivals. On the Hobbesian
conception this is because, if the state strayed from legal responses, it
would plunge the community into precisely the 'warre of every man
against every man' that terrifies Hobbesians. That would destroy the
community through removing the source of order on which its common
life depends.

For Hobbes, broadly speaking, the existence of any state is to the
overwhelming advantage of its citizens, who are therefore quite unjustified in seeking to overthrow it by violence. The democratic theory which
underpins the Political Crime model of terrorism does not share that view.
It accepts that the consequence of overthrowing the state is the breaking up
of the community. But it supposes that some may be so disadvantaged by
a particular state system as to be better off without it. A new state with these
individuals in a dominant position may emerge. Arguments against violent
opposition are available only in a democratic state that can fairly consider
the claims of different interest groups. Any other kind of state is potentially
unstable and lacks the degree of social cohesion that adherence to democratically agreed rules can provide.

To examine these conceptions we need to consider more carefully what
a community is, and how it relates to its form of government. Political
philosophers (for example Raphael 1974: 32–4) sometimes introduce the
notion of community by way of Tönnies' famous distinction between
Gemeinschaft and *Gesellschaft*: between community and association.[4] In
Tönnies' sense a community is a social group not formed for a definite
purpose or deliberately organized to that end, but valued for its own sake
and entered into in a way that expresses what Tönnies calls 'natural will'.
An association by contrast is formed for an explicit purpose and organized
to attain it: it thus expresses 'rational will'. Tönnies thought of families,
groups of friends and so forth as communities. For our purposes we need
to use the expression 'community' to name groups whose members share
a less limited range of common concerns, as do the inhabitants of villages
beyond the commuter belt for example. Within such a community there
may be many associations: the local branch of the Agricultural Workers'
Union, the church choir and so on.

When the community is taken to comprise the inhabitants of a certain country, many philosophers suppose that among the associations the adult members enter is that country's state. The purpose of the state is, it is said (for example Raphael 1974: 46), 'to prevent and settle conflict' and it has a specific organization to achieve this, in which some of its members are liable for conscription, jury service and other conflict-settling tasks. It is easy to fall into thinking of the state as simply a well supported neighbourhood watch association writ large. Yet this is to overlook the comprehensive scope of the state's regulatory activities. Like other associations, a neighbourhood watch association has rules binding upon its members relevant to its purpose of preventing assault and theft. The state's rules, however, do not concern only how to enforce the law. They are the law. So while a neighbourhood watch association does not make the rules forbidding assault and theft, the modern state, like some more zealous vigilante association, does do just that. On the Hobbesian conception we can make no distinction between the state and the community here. If the state is an association which aims to maintain order among its members through enforcing its rules then there is really no place for talking of the community as well. Without that association, there would be only an aggregate of individuals, not a community.

The Hobbesian conception stands in sharp contrast to the conception of a community as determined by shared rules for living a common life. There need be no clear purposes in a community that its rules serve to fulfil, though there can be no common living without rules of social interaction. But only if one was convinced that there was a terrifying alternative to common life – 'the warre of every man against every man' – would one think that those rules were formulated expressly with the purpose of preventing incipient disorder. On the Communitarian conception, the preservation of order in the community is here equated with the application of rules for common living. It is not a separately specifiable goal which they subserve. In a community, as so understood, it is best to think of the state as the civil power or government which enforces some of these rules.

If we wish to use Tönnies' distinction to characterize the social and political structures of a land, then we must use it as he did, to distinguish, not two types of social structure co-present within a country at a time, but two types of structure within which the inhabitants might fall at different times. At one time we might have a community, with its government; and at another the state, construed as a political association. These are, as Tönnies put it (1971: 155), 'ideal types'. At most times the social structure will not fall easily into either. Indeed, it seems to me that this is precisely our present situation.

It is, however, very much in the interests of the modern state to view itself as an association, and to make that a criterion of communal identity. For it is only when citizens regard the possibility of a common life as dependent upon their membership of a particular political association that a desire for social cohesion can be translated into loyalty to a state.

V

A democratic state may go further and claim legitimacy as a political association on the basis of its democratic structures. This is consonant with the equation drawn in the Political Crime model of terrorism between legitimacy and the availability of channels for dealing with dissent, which are allegedly provided by democracy. Yet upon consideration it is far from clear that the fact that an association has democratic methods for making its rules does anything to show that it is legitimate, that it is the proper association for pursuing the goals at which it aims.

Similarly with the state. The legitimacy of the state as the proper body to maintain order in a particular territory is not something that can be established by a majority vote of the members of the state. For what such a majority cannot decide is who shall vote to decide who the members of the state shall be. This criticism of the notion that the popular sovereignty deriving from democratic procedures somehow confers legitimacy is nicely put by Ivor Jennings (quoted in French and Gutman 1974: 138): 'On the surface it seemed reasonable: let the people decide. It was in fact ridiculous because the people cannot decide until somebody decides who the people are'. Where there is a dispute over that – as in the North of Ireland – it is evident that it cannot be resolved by the existing membership. A majority in the Six Counties is in favour of the union with Great Britain. It is evident there is a majority of the people of Ireland as a whole in favour of a united Ireland. The matter rests ultimately in the hands of the United Kingdom, though it is doubtful what a majority vote on it there would opt for. This highlights a grave defect in the theory of the democratic state: the democratic process can provide no criterion as to which groups should constitute separate states. Since a grievance over this kind of question cannot be resolved democratically, the arguments against terrorism implied by the Political Crime view fall away when terrorists claim that a state with a given membership is not a legitimate political entity.

It is for just this reason that it is so often in disputes over statehood that terrorism is resorted to. Those who have a grievance on such questions may have no alternative but to resort to the military means of replacing the state involved in terrorism.

The inevitability of this damaging conclusion has been disputed. Harry Beran, for example, has recently argued for recognizing the right of secession. He says (1987: 37) it 'is required by the value democratic liberalism places on freedom, by a liberal democratic theory of popular sovereignty, and by a presupposition of legitimate majority rule'. In other words, he claims, first, that the idea of the voluntariness of human relationships must be applied to the unity of the state; second, that popular 'sovereignty must be composed of the moral rights of individuals to decide their political relationships'; and, third, that majority votes are only binding where there is agreement to accept them (unless a minority *cannot* leave the group). Accordingly Beran holds that potential separatists must be allowed a vote on secession in the areas for which they are proposing it.

Such views were noted by Henry Sidgwick many years ago. On the 'indefinite disintegration of political societies' to which an unrestricted right of secession might lead, Sidgwick (1891: 621–22) observed that 'some of those who hold that a government, to be legitimate, must rest on the consent of the governed, appear not to shrink from drawing this inference; they appear to qualify the right of the majority of members of a state to rule by allowing the claim of a minority that suffers from the exercise of this right to secede and form a new state, when it is in a majority in a continuous portion of its old state's territory'. Sidgwick himself would severely curtail this alleged right to secede to cases where 'some unjust sacrifice or grossly incompetent management of their interests, or some persistent and harsh opposition to their legitimate desires' existed, as against cases where merely 'the interests of the seceders would be promoted or their sentiments of nationality gratified by the change' (Ibid.: 271).

Although Sidgwick writes from a utilitarian standpoint he persistently raises questions of justice and injustice to the parties in dispute over secession which are ignored by Beran. In doing so he presupposes the existence of continuing communities, behind the structure of states, with claims on and obligations to those who would secede from them. For Beran, by contrast, there are only on the one hand states as units of social organization, and on the other individuals living in a particular place and thereby having coincident interests, which differ perhaps from those of individuals living elsewhere and which are best served by a distinct organization.

It is arguable that Beran's view is what is required when the Hobbesian conception of the state is wedded to the theory of popular sovereignty exercised through majority rule. In reply to Beran's three arguments, it needs to be said, however, first, that freedom of association is itself subject to state control in the interests of order. Second, it is clear that on the Hobbesian view we cannot regard sovereignty of the people as exercisable except collectively, and by 'the generation of that great LEVIATHAN ... to which we owe our peace and defence' (Hobbes 1962: pt 2, ch. 17): thus sovereignty consists in power, not in 'the moral rights of individuals to decide their political relationships'. Nor, thirdly, is it evident what room there is for making the binding force of majority votes depend on their acceptance, when to refuse to accept them is to claim more than an equal democratic share in decision-making. But if one is impressed by these counterarguments one may have to accept that no justification in the will of majorities can be given for the particular state associations that there are. They exist as associations for preserving order until they come peaceably or violently apart, but no argument can be adduced from their democratic organization to dissuade those who seek to come together differently from violence to that end.

VI

The Hobbesian view, even when wedded to democratic theory, provides us with no criterion of a single political community independent of its statehood. An aspiration to statehood from a group's sense of already being a distinct community, as against the desire of individual members to associate differently, has no place in the theory. However, it is not immediately clear that the anti-Hobbesian conception of community can provide for an aspiration to statehood either. For even if that conception is able to provide a criterion for being a single political community it has no obvious account of why such a community should aspire to statehood, that is to have a single and exclusive government, rather than being content with any government so long as it administers its rules, as medieval political theory suggests it should. On this conception, terrorists who fight a war to protect their community from the injustices of tyrannical govern-ment may seem to be justified only so long as they do not go on to fight to achieve separate statehood for it. A version of this view has been put forward with respect to the IRA claim to fight a Just War in the North of Ireland (Simpson 1986: 73–88; see Gilbert 1987: 217–21). On this view the suppression of a community's aspiration to independent rule would not constitute injustice, since the community's identity does not depend on its form of government.

Yet although the Communitarian theory, unlike its Hobbesian rival, allows no *a priori* link between communal identity and form of government, it does not need to deny that there may in practice be such links. Here medieval and modern versions of the theory can part company. While the medieval theory seems to assume *a priori* that a community is identifiable whether or not there is a ruler to enforce its rules, a modern version, like Engels's, can hold that it is an empirical matter to what extent communal identity depends on the requirements of obedience to a particular government. Obedience to a government can undermine the rules governing relationships in virtue of which a single community was once identified. Obedience to a foreign government can threaten the indigenous community.

Now it becomes apparent that other grounds for challenge to the legitimacy of governments to rule within a land are available, apart from lack of consent. Vague as it is, the claim that a form of government is undermining communal identity is a common justification for separatist campaigns. Those in Scotland and Wales provide local examples. Independent government may, to an extent, protect communal identity since one does not need to have a Hobbesian conception to allow that without a supporting state it may be lost. The contrasting Communitarian conception underlies, I suspect, most separatist struggles. It provides *prima facie*, as democratic theory does not, some rationale for statehood.

What the Communitarian conception requires is that relations other than those of power relations vis-à-vis the state should be able to determine communal identity. These are essentially reciprocal relations in which members recognize the claims each has on the others in pursuit of a common interest. These reciprocally recognized claims are embodied in the rules of the community. The common interest normally generated by living together in the same place is not restricted to the avoidance of conflict between members but extends to whatever is required for living together well. It is the rules for promoting this, often as vague and unspoken as are the aims they serve, whose scope determines a community. It is breaches of the rules that may call for the use of coercive power. But the existence of the rules is an expression of reciprocity, not of power relations; of mutual agreement, not of individual submission.

A community so construed will commonly seek *self*-government, since the existence of coercive power inevitably creates the possibility that the interests of those wielding it will be advanced at the expense of the community as a whole. This risk can be removed only if the community as a whole has control over state power. It is evident that the interests of the community as a whole may differ from the individual interests of a subgroup, even of a majority one (see Rousseau 1968: bk 2, ch 3). In such a situation the community as a whole may suffer even where there is democratic government. The community may, for example, be divided between advantaged and disadvantaged sections. Here again the state's claim to legitimacy may be challenged on behalf of the community. This broadly speaking is what provides a motive for the kind of challenge to legitimacy that counts as revolution.

The Communitarian conception provides for the possibility that civil strife may actually *restore* cohesion to a society whose reciprocal bonds have been loosened by alien or coercive government, or bring communal relations where they were not enjoyed before. This may seem a romantic picture. It is, I suggest, a necessary antidote to the Hobbesian view. Internal terrorism should lead us to re-examine our relations with those of our fellow citizens who seek to wage war against the existing state. Questions about what pattern of communal relations is due to them cannot be sensibly discussed if we view ourselves as defending the possibility of society itself. Here the words of Henry Sidgwick (1891: 621) nearly a century ago are still pertinent:

> I think it important to dispel the illusion that any form of government can ever give a complete security against civil war. Such a security, if attained, must rest on a moral rather than a political basis; it must be maintained by the moderation and justice, the comprehensive sympathies and enlightened public spirit, of the better citizens, keeping within bounds the fanaticism of sects, the cupidities of classes, and the violence of victorious partisanship; it cannot be found in any supposed moral right of a numerical majority of persons inhabiting any part of the earth's surface, to be obeyed by the minority who live within the same district.[5]

Notes

1. See Mrs Thatcher's Guildhall Speech, 14 November 1988. In the context of discussing the justification of a 'war against terrorism' I exclude consideration of 'state terrorism', which may be employed in such a 'war'.
2. I have explored this theme at greater length in Gilbert 1989.
3. Even if the community is self-governing the Communitarian conception will still allow the Just War theorist a distinction between someone *qua* member of the community and *qua* participant in rule. Only in the latter role could he be a legitimate target.

4. See Tönnies 1971: esp. 131 ff. (The translators speak of 'essential' and 'arbitrary' rather than 'natural' and 'rational will', as Raphael does.)
5. I should like to thank my colleagues Kathleen Lennon and Gerry Wallace for valuable discussion.

PART I
Terrorism

2. Reflections on Terrorism and Violence

Anthony Quinton

I

What more is there to terrorism than violence?

All terrorism is necessarily violent, but violence is not necessarily terrorism. A madman who takes up a point of vantage and promiscuously shoots anyone who comes within range is not a terrorist. Nor is a bank robber who kills in pursuit of private gain. Nor again is a woman who kills her husband after a long period of maltreatment or to be free to go off with a more attractive lover. Nor is a man who drunkenly assaults with a broken bottle someone whose appearance he dislikes.

In some of these cases of nonterrorist violence there is an absence of clear and thought-out purpose behind the violent acts involved. Unlike the madman and the drunkard the terrorist acts violently in a deliberate way. In the cases of the bank robber and the two wives, while the violence is deliberate, the purposes to which it is directed are private and personal. To be terrorism violence has to have a political end.

In holding that terrorism is violence that has a political purpose I am not saying that the violence in question has to be politically motivated to any preponderating extent for its perpetrator. A member of a politically motivated group who takes part merely because he likes killing people or blowing things up is still a terrorist, because his violent action is part of the declared and, for the most part sincerely, politically motivated violent activity of the group. He is, perhaps, a parasitic terrorist. But the context in which he operates distinguishes him from someone who kills or maims other people for pleasure or private revenge or for no clear reason at all, on his own.

The application of the word *terrorist* will vary with the sense of the word *political*. Suppose a very rough trade union tried to strengthen its case that the safety precautions of the employers were inadequate by

35

pushing a few people into the machinery. Although the conflict in question is economic rather than strictly political, the violence imagined is still surely terroristic. There is also the case of enthusiasts for animal rights who blow up a laboratory in which vivisection is being practised. Their purpose is likely to be primarily moral, to prevent what they take to be the morally bad things done by animal experimenters, and not the political and more indirect goal of inducing the government to enact, or the public to demand, legislation forbidding experiments on animals. The appropriate qualification, then, should be that terrorism is violence directed towards a public or social end rather than to a private or personal one or, *a fortiori,* to no end at all beyond the act itself.

But that does not go far enough. There is a great deal of publicly or socially directed violence that is not terrorism. Rioters, who seek to demonstrate their convictions in a public, noisy way or to occupy buildings or to destroy the hated symbols of whatever it is that they dislike, are likely to be ready for violence and, even, to intend it. But it is not an essential part of their project that the level of violence should be very high, that it should extend to killing or seriously wounding the police or whoever it may be who seeks to bar their passage through the streets or into the prison. Violence is something that is likely to happen, and may be confidently expected to happen, as a consequence of something else which it is their primary intention to do. If it fails to materialize they may well be disappointed. But rioters are not, as such, terrorists. This is because if rioting does give rise to serious violence it is a contingent matter and also to a considerable extent reactive, not something the rioters themselves initiate.

A similar case is that of the conscious and deliberate participant in an organized revolutionary upheaval. To march with arms in hand on the presidential palace is clearly to be ready for violence in pursuit of a political end. But here again the violence involved is contingent and reactive. Provided that the aim of overthrowing the government is achieved the organizers of the event may well be pleased if there is no bloodshed. The storming of the Bastille was a great success in spite of the very low level of violence involved. The intention to kill or injure seriously is an essential part of terrorism in a way that it is not essential to revolution.

It may be objected that a very familiar kind of politically motivated conduct which is universally described as terrorism is hijacking, or hostage-taking in general. In this line of activity the threat of serious violence is used to compel such things as the release of political prisoners. But, like the revolutionary, the hijacker aims at something that does not essentially involve the use of serious violence. His purpose can be fully realized if no such violence is done. Hijackings, indeed, like revolutions, very often involve a good deal of serious violence. But both – hijacking particularly – are more successful if they do not. Hijackers are usually people who would qualify as terrorists on other grounds, while the majority of revolutionaries do not have or need the special qualities of character needed for any chance of success in enterprises of hijacking or of what would be described without hesitation as terrorism. Is it this, or is it the fact that hijacking and straightforward terrorism are, in contrast to full-blooded revolution, small-scale affairs, and thus more capable of being prepared in secrecy, which brings them together and distinguishes them from revolution?

A more substantial underlying consideration is that in hijacking or hostage-taking, as in straightforward terrorism, the victims of violence or the threat of it are passive in a way that governments under threat of revolution are not. A government is prepared for its own defence. To anticipate a point to be considered more broadly later, from a certain point of view the business of the state is violence; that of airline passengers and of Northern Irish pub customers is, ordinarily, not. Furthermore, what the revolutionaries want from the governments they confront, the concession of power or authority, is something those governments are in a position to provide if they choose to. The hapless occupants of hijacked airliners or Northern Irish pubs can themselves do nothing to release political prisoners or end the partition of Ireland.

Is a saboteur a terrorist? Many of the things which it is attractive to the saboteur to destroy – bridges, barracks, railway lines, public buildings – are commonly occupied by people for most or much of the time. Bombing or burning these places implies a readiness to kill or maim anyone present. Here again the human victims of the saboteur's actions, although their death or serious injury is, as in the case of revolution, not essential to the achievement of the saboteur's aim, are, as in the case of hijacking, passive. The violence inflicted on them is in no way causally involved with their defence of themselves against attack. This aligns the saboteur with the hijacker, as a kind of terrorist, and distinguishes him from the straightforward participant in a revolution.

Hijacking, hostage-taking and sabotage are reasonably associated with the more central or paradigmatic varieties of terrorism, even if serious violence is not essential to them, but only the threat of it in the first two cases, while it is likely in all of them. In all of them the victims of violence, actual or possible, are passive means to the realization of ends which they are themselves in no position to promote. With assassination, on the other hand, the death or disabling injury of the targeted victim is essential to the success of the undertaking, and not a contingent by-product of it, just because he is seen as a causally influential support of the state of affairs the assassin wishes to transform.

There is a significant difference between assassination and what may be regarded as the purest form of terrorism. Pure terrorism is random and arbitrary; its unpredictable character makes it difficult to take precautions against it. Assassination is directed at specific targets, seen either as important elements of resistance to the political aims of the terrorist or as a potent symbol of that resistance: a prime minister, for example, in the first case; a constitutional monarch in the second.

No sharp boundary separates assassination from pure terrorism. The killing or maiming of ordinary soldiers or policemen, who fall between the importance of political leaders and generals and the anonymity of the victims of pure terrorism, is not clearly one thing or the other.

Hooliganism – now, as in the Falstaffian past, one of the less distinguished British contributions to European civilization – is of too much current interest to be neglected in a discussion of violence. Hooligans quite often have a diffuse political commitment, a kind of primitive nationalism, expressed in the wearing and waving of Union Jacks and principally composed of hatred of foreigners and contempt for them. But there is no further determinate purpose to it beyond that of inspiring fear of British mobs among those intruded upon. This is a marginal, low-grade kind of terrorism, placed somewhere between the purposeless violence of the maniac on the loose with a rifle and terrorism proper. It should in fairness be added that the level of violence intended by hooligans is not very high, as the comparative mildness of their weapons – knives, chains, iron bars and so forth – makes clear. Where it does lead to large numbers of deaths, as at the Heysel Stadium, such an outcome is neither planned nor expected.

A terrorist is a kind of unofficial soldier. While the general who plans the combatant activities of the front-line soldiery is a soldier too, the noncombatant organizers or impresarios of terrorism like Gaddafi and Khomeini are not themselves literally describable as terrorists. The reason for this is no doubt the fact that for the most part terrorist groups are small, so that those who plan and control their violent acts themselves take part in them.

All I have been doing so far is to delineate, with a bit more explicit detail than is usual, the everyday concept of the terrorist. I am not claiming that the concept is above criticism, only that it is familiar, unitary and internally coherent. It takes a terrorist to be one who pursues a public, social or political end by means to which physical violence is essential. I have further assumed, but not yet discussed, the condition that the terrorist's violence is not part of the official operations of the state.

Objections can be raised to the seriousness or significance of this conception on the ground that some of the distinguishing features of terrorism on which it relies mark differences which are of no real importance. There is a real and objective difference between thefts committed by people with surnames beginning with the letters from A to L and those committed by people whose names begin with the letters from M to Z. But it is an utterly insignificant difference on which it would be absurd to base different attitudes to the two groups discriminated. It would be absurd, more specifically, if the pejorative force of the word *theft* were preserved for the A to L thefts but not for the M to Z thefts. The objections I have in mind to the everyday notion of terrorism I have roughly defined are of this general nature. The first is that there is no serious difference between physical violence and other kinds of violence sufficient to justify a difference of attitude to them. The second is that there is no serious difference between the unofficial violence singled out by the conventional notion of terrorism and the violence that is carried out officially by states and which is, indeed, an essential ingredient in the concept of the state.

II

Must violence be physical?

I shall not spend very much time on the contention that not all violence is literal, physical violence, bodily assault calculated to kill, mutilate or wound. Even if it were acceptable it would have little bearing on the matter in hand. Those who say that bad housing, or any other defective aspect of the human condition, is violence would not, presumably, want to go on to say that a slum landlord who does nothing to keep his property in decent condition or an employer who turns people out of work by introducing labour-saving machinery is really a terrorist.

The doctrine that bad housing or unemployment or malnutrition is violence is an example of the Madeline Bassett school of political thought. She is reported by Bertie Wooster as saying that rabbits are gnomes in attendance on the Fairy Queen and that the stars are God's daisy chain. Wooster quite correctly comments, 'Perfect rot, of course. They are nothing of the sort' (Wodehouse 1953: 12). What she no doubt meant was that the stars were like God's daisy chain or made her think of it. In the same spirit, the statement that bad housing is violence may be understood as a rhetorically overexcited way of saying that it is *as bad as* violence.

That very broad contention is deficient in several ways. In the first place, bad housing and violence are not very comparable, except in the very general respects that both are bad for the people who undergo them and that both, unlike earthquakes and brain tumours, are avoidable or preventable. A crucial difference is that violence is something that people inflict in a positive, intentional fashion on others and bad housing is not. Those who fail to prevent the literal violence of people other than themselves are not guilty of violence, though they may be blameable for dereliction of duty, if, for example, they are policemen aware of and close to the violence in question. The deliberate infliction of bad housing on people is hardly imaginable as a serious possibility in the way that simply letting them endure it is. There are speculative builders who put up cheap housing that is likely to deteriorate in a short time if not energetically maintained. But they do not compel anyone to live in the rubbish they build. If anything does, it is the circumstances, in a metaphorical way, of the people who find themselves living there because there is no alternative available to them. For these and other reasons it is not easy to compare the two things, just as it is not easy to compare a stroke and bankruptcy. Violence and bad housing can vary in all sorts of relevant ways: violence as more or less severe, housing as more or less awful, both as affecting more or fewer people. There is really no sense to the idea that in general one is as bad as the other.

More important, however, is the consideration that the prevention of violent conflict between individuals and of the infliction of violence by some individuals on others has always been the primary task of the state, along with the protection of the citizenry from violent assault from outside the state's borders. It is not just a historical peculiarity that states first arose as institutions to prevent or resist violence, internal or external. It remains their first responsibility, one which cannot be discharged in any other way and such that if it is not discharged with reasonable effectiveness everything else human beings prize and depend on is put at risk. Bad housing can be lived with; uncontrolled violence cannot. Bad housing can be overcome or circumvented in many ways; only the state can control violence.

The only rapidly effective way of controlling violence – realistically, the only effective way, fast or slow – is the use or threat of violence by the state. The point is made in the idiom of Madeline Bassett by Merleau-Ponty (1969: xxxvi) when he says 'all law is violence'. It is made in more grown-up language by Weber (1946: 78) when he defines the state as 'a political association [that] successfully upholds a claim to the monopoly of the use of physical force'. This raises the question, deferred until now: why should the word *terrorism*, with its pejorative quality, be confined to unofficial violence, to violence not carried out or threatened by the state?

III

Is state violence terrorism?

An answer that goes a fairly long way towards replying adequately to this question is that in reasonably orderly and well established states the amount of actual violence that the state and its agents exercise on its citizens (to prevent them from being violent to one another, first of all, but also for the enforcement of law generally) is extremely small. Most arrests are peaceful; defendants on the whole behave calmly in court; they do not have to be physically coerced to go to prison when they are sentenced.

Furthermore, orderly and well established states do offer actual violence to their citizens only when those citizens themselves act violently towards the agents of the state, in resisting arrest, for example, or towards other citizens, in, for instance, the streets of Hungerford or a football stadium, or both, as at a miners' picket line. Internally, at any rate, in normal, peaceable circumstances, intentional violence on the part of the state does not amount to terrorism in an official guise, any more than that of anyone who might have fired back at Michael Ryan. Such violence as there is is reactive, a matter of self-defence.

But there are two varieties of official violence which, since not reactive or defensive, are much more like terrorism. The first is that of states which act violently towards nonviolent opposition, sending Cossacks or tanks into action against peaceful demonstrations. This is an obscure region because the peaceful or nonviolent character of the demonstrations may, on the one hand, be spurious, a show put on by their organizers to attract support and conceal their real intentions, or, on the other, alter because of the familiar tendency of large mobs of people to become violent in a way few of their members would have been if not crowded together. The second kind of case, in which states come closest to terrorism in the conventional sense which I have tried to set out, is that in which random or arbitrary violence is used to ensure the submission of the public to whatever the state decrees, however unwelcome. Stalin's terror is at once the purest and the

most massive example of this form of state policy. At first it had more of
the character of assassination, being directed against declared opponents
of and potential rebels against the regime. But it extended to take in anyone
the dictator and his police chiefs of the moment chose to fasten on and
derived added force as a means of intimidation from doing so. Hitler's
terror seems to have remained for the most part at the earlier, directed,
nonrandom stage, at least so far as Germans were concerned. Even his
assault on the Jews was nonrandom to the extent that he can be credited
with genuinely accepting the grotesque beliefs about Jews which he
professed.

Most states, however well ordered and established they may be, and so
however minimal the violence they actually use against their own citizens,
are, at least intermittently, very violent towards the citizens of other states.
Warfare, even in its most mercenary and chess-like form, necessarily
involves the threat of violence and in all its postdynastic, national forms,
a high level of actual violence. At all times those not themselves directly
offering violence to the forces of another nation have been violently
handled by them. In the early modern period this effect of warfare was
largely casual and contingent, a by-product of armies provisioning themselves by pillage, although often a deliberate policy, designed to weaken
resistance. In our age it is a consequence of the specially destructive
character of modern weapons.

Even when not openly at war, states seek to damage their enemies by
inciting resistance among the citizens of the enemy state or by conducting
or financing violent activity against it within its borders. It is the extent to
which he claims to discern this kind of thing in American policy towards
Latin American and Asian countries to whose regimes the United States is
opposed that leads Chomsky (1978: 59; 66; 76) to describe that policy as
one of terror.

Much of what is conventionally regarded as terrorism is nationalistic
in inspiration: that of the IRA, the Basque ETA, the various Palestinian
organizations. They try to legitimize their violence by claiming that it is no
more than warfare on behalf of an oppressed nation. Where some would
regard soldiers as terrorists with pension arrangements, they see themselves as soldiers without uniforms. In some cases, such as that of the IRA,
the claim is pretty hollow. There already exists a predominantly Catholic
and sovereign Irish state which is not at war with the United Kingdom, even
if it shares, in a diluted and more or less ceremonial way, the professed aim
of the IRA, to bring the Six Counties of the North under the control of that
state. The fact that the IRA commands quite a lot of sympathy among the

citizens of the Irish Republic does not lend very much colour to the IRA's claims. Unwillingness to see compatriots fall into the hands of the traditional oppressor does not amount to an abandonment of loyalty to the actual Republic of Ireland and a transfer of allegiance to the imaginary state of the IRA.

The historical indications are that terrorism is often successful – or, at any rate, associated with success – in the realization of its nationalistic aims. De Valera in Ireland, Begin and Shamir in Israel came to lead the independent nation-states on whose behalf they had become terrorists. But it does not always succeed. Macedonia remains cut up in pieces.

For the ordinary loyal citizens of a state that is at the receiving end of terrorism there is the problem of reconciling morally indignant endorsement of forceful response to terrorist outrage with connivance with the use of terror by their own state in support of interests less important and compelling than its own identity. In practice the possession of clean hands does not act as a protection against terrorism. The first and overriding responsibility of a state to its own citizens is to protect them against violence, not least at the hands of foreigners. That protection is more acceptable if it is not itself randomly terroristic.

It is not simply a matter of moral consistency. Some have blamed the current prevalence of terrorism on the widespread adoption of ethical consequentialism. But ethical consequentialism is not uncritical about either means or ends. In particular, it does not support the assumption of the identity of a particular nation as overriding all other moral considerations. The level of oppression to be removed by national independence has to be rationally estimated. So has its likelihood as contrasted with the certain evil of the terrorist policies adopted to achieve it. The violence of the Irgun and the Stern gang should be measured against the sufferings of the Jews under Hitler. Beside them those of the Catholics of Northern Ireland or the Basques of northern Spain do not bulk large. Wherever national independence has been achieved by means among which terrorism was included the question always arises: could the result have been achieved just as well without it?

3. Some Observations on the Relationships between Terrorism and Freedom

Paul Wilkinson

The concept of terrorism

Most political–strategic concepts are slippery and elude easy definition. But that does not mean that we cannot or should not use them. For example, the vocabulary of philosophical and political debate would be considerably impoverished if we abandoned concepts such as 'imperialism', 'war' and 'revolution'.[1] The notion that we should be aiming to restrict ourselves to using a strictly 'value-free' language of politics is based on a fundamental mistake.[2] We cannot escape the context of our own humanity, values, beliefs and experience. Nor can we use our concepts meaningfully unless we relate them to a specific context.

I readily admit that my own understanding of the meaning of terrorism is shaped by my own preference for liberal democratic values[3] and my experience of living and working in a liberal democratic society. However, it is worth noting that there is now a widely shared common understanding and usage of the concept of terrorism among scholars, lawyers, governments and the educated public in the liberal democratic societies generally (see Jenkins 1980: 3–10). Thus, when a French politician or jurist talks to an American colleague about terrorist phenomena there is no fundamental conceptual barrier to effective communication. (They may differ concerning the facts of an alleged terrorist incident, or regarding the appropriate political or judicial measures that should be taken, but this is a very different set of problems.)[4] There is a very widely shared consensus among Western 'liberal' states that terrorism is not a synonym for violence in general; rather, it is a special mode or method of violence which can be used either in isolation, or as part of a wider repertoire of conflict, for example in conjunction with rural guerrilla warfare, economic disruption, riots, and so on. It is clear that terrorism can be utilized both by subnational actors and by states for an unlimited variety of ideological, political, religious and criminal aims and purposes. Briefly defined, terrorism is the deliberate and systematic use of coercive intimidation to create a climate of extreme fear among a wider target group than the immediate victims of the violence. Terrorism has been used for a wide range of purposes. It can attempt to coerce sections of the population and/or governments into making concessions or submitting to the perpetrators' will or demands. Terrorists utilize the mass media to convey and intensify the sense of fear and insecurity among the public at large or its chosen target groups. Terrorism provides a kind of gruesome theatre of atrocity, and its perpetrators frequently seek to exploit the public outrage they hope to engender either to frighten members of the public into withdrawing active cooperation and support from the government or other opposing groups, or to provoke the authorities into overreacting with draconian measures which the terrorists expect will swell support for their own cause (Jenkins 1974).

It is frequently suggested that the usage of the concept of terrorism outlined above is so contentious or 'value-loaded' that there is no adequate basis for meaningful scholarly debate and collaborative research in the field.[5] This is far from being the case. Since the mid 1970s there has been considerable development internationally in the academic social scientific and historical literature on terrorism. As one would expect there is an enormous variety of approaches, theories and methodologies within the field. An examination of the scholarly literature on other aspects of conflict, such as revolution or limited war, would find a similar diversity of methods and conclusions. It would be foolish to expect the literature on terrorism to reflect total agreement on concepts, theories, data and literature. It is noteworthy, however, that the most authoritative guide to the international literature on terrorism (Schmid 1988) concludes that there is a consensus among over a hundred leading scholars worldwide on what its editors call a 'minimal definition' of terrorism. This consensus rests on five elements or characteristics which the overwhelming majority of scholars in the field identify as the distinguishing characteristics or hallmarks of terroristic violence. These five elements are:

1. the intention to create extreme fear or terror;
2. the targeting of random and symbolic targets, including civilians and civilian property;
3. the attempt to influence a wider audience than the immediate victims of the violence;

4. the use of particularly brutal or extreme methods of violence, viewed as 'extranormal' according to the norms of the community under attack;
5. the exploitation of terrorism for a variety of purposes, including influencing the mass media, public opinion, sectors of the population and governments .

It is this widely accepted conceptualization of terrorism which is employed in the present paper.

II

'Freedom fighters' and 'soldiers of national liberation'

The vast majority of contemporary perpetrators of the special mode of violence described above totally reject the appellation 'terrorist'. They portray themselves as freedom fighters or soldiers of national liberation struggles or warriors of revolution. It is easy to understand why they view the terrorist label as bad for their image. The concept of terrorism undoubtedly carries with it the clearly pejorative implications of illegitimacy and indiscriminate brutality against civilian targets. Terrorist movements naturally prefer to portray themselves as heroic fighters for a noble cause. In their eyes they are waging a righteous war. Because it is a war which is sanctified and legitimated by their ideological beliefs, they are supremely confident that the end justifies their means. Thus they repeatedly describe themselves as engaging in 'military operations' against their 'enemy', the hated oppressor.

But just suppose that redressing the denial of national self-determination is genuinely the underlying motive of the movement utilizing terrorism. Does this legitimate the use of terrorist means to that end? Surely not, because the waging of a just war of liberation against an alien conqueror does not necessarily or inevitably involve a deliberate waging of terror, a systematic policy of murder and massacre against the civilian population.[6] Indeed the use of such methods, whether on the part of insurgent movements or the armed forces of states, is explicitly prohibited by the International Humanitarian Law (IHL) as contained in the Geneva Conventions and the 1977 Protocols.[7] And while it is certainly the case that these rules of war have been violated on numerous occasions, this does not mean that the IHL regime, so fragile but so necessary for some minimum protection of human rights in times of war, can or should be cavalierly discarded. All states and insurgent movements which recognize the Geneva IHL code have an obligation to obey its rules, and can be called to account for breaches of the conventions. Terrorist movements, however, scathingly dismiss the restraints of international humanitarian law as so much 'bourgeois sentimentality'.[8] They see any attempt to impose such constraints on them as a Machiavellian attempt to rob them of their flexibility and scope for employing terrorist methods, which they see as an essential means to compensate for lack of conventional military resources and manpower. This helps to explain the terrorists' total rejection of legal and humanitarian constraints, the view so candidly expressed by one notorious modern terrorist movement, that 'armed struggle has no limits'.[9]

Terrorists' claims to be waging a struggle for the ultimate goal of freedom may in some cases be shown to be genuine. From a liberal democratic perspective, for example, the objective of achieving a free and democratic independent Palestinian state would seem entirely worthy. (Let us leave aside, for a moment, the problem that some groups, such as the PFLP, seek to establish a Marxist–Leninist state of Palestine which would contain all the features of a 'democratic centralist' dictatorship.)[10]

However, in the vast majority of cases the claim of the terrorists that they are a legitimate national liberation movement can be shown to be entirely spurious. For example, the claim of the Basque terrorist movement, ETA, that it is the authentic representative of the Basque people can be shown to be nonsense (Pollack and Hunter 1988: 139–42). The electoral support that the pro-terrorist political party, Herri Batasuna, achieved in the 1984 autonomous elections was only one in ten of the Basque adult population. It has now (1989) dropped still further. Indeed, the largest ever political demonstrations in Western Europe since 1945 have been by Basques angrily protesting against ETA violence in rallies and marches in the Basque cities. The Libyan-backed Provisional IRA in Northern Ireland also makes spurious claims to legitimacy.[11] Yet the PIRA's political party, Provisional Sinn Fein, cannot even win a majority of the votes of the Catholic minority of the Province – a clear case of a terrorist movement claiming to want to 'liberate' a people that does not want to be liberated by the PIRA under any terms.[12]

III

Is it possible to be a 'freedom fighter' in an operative liberal democracy?

In any truly operative liberal democracy there are, by definition, always means and channels of voicing protest and campaigning for change by nonviolent means. For example, in both the Basque region of Spain and the Province of Northern Ireland there are free elections, universal suffrage, freedoms of worship and opinion, and freedom to organize and belong to political parties. The ethnic minority populations are not in any way excluded from these rights and freedoms. Thus there can be no possible justification for the terrorist groups' use of murder, maiming and the destruction of property. They have ample democratic channels open to them to achieve the political expression of their policies and aims.

And even if these democratic freedoms did not already exist, it would be ridiculous to argue that the only way of achieving them, or of changing society, is by terrorism. In every case in the past quarter of a century where democratic rights have been gained and dictatorship undermined, this betterment has been achieved by means other than terrorism. In Greece, Portugal and Spain the ending of dictatorships came through popular pressure and protest on the streets. In the Philippines, the Marcos dictatorship was overthrown by a combination of popular democratic will and American pressure.

One is therefore bound to conclude that the freedom the terrorists within a liberal democracy are really seeking is not 'freedom' in the democratic sense of the term, but rather their *own* freedom to use the gun and the bomb in an effort to impose their own petty minority tyranny on the majority, because they have been forced to recognize that they cannot win support for their ideas through the ballot box. Thus terrorists waging violence against their fellow citizens and the legal and constitutional organs in a liberal democratic state are only 'freedom fighters' in their own eyes, not by any objective criteria, such as electoral support or generally recognized status of moral right or legitimacy. The 'freedom' they pursue in reality is the perversion of the freedoms made possible by the democratic state. In other words, they exploit the freedoms of the open society the better to pursue their effort to terrorize the society and its government into submitting to their demands. They use their own freedom to abuse the most fundamental rights of their fellows, the rights to life, liberty and happiness, and the right to live in peace and freedom under the rule of law. It is also important to observe that the pursuit of terrorist violence has an inexorably self-corrupting and criminalizing effect on the individual terrorists[13] as they become enmeshed in conspiracy to murder and destroy, and the underworld activities such as armed robbery and racketeering which they habitually use to sustain their organizations (see Adams 1985). For them 'freedom' is the freedom of the Mafia, in reality the insatiable appetite for maintaining a 'free market' in organized crime.

IV

A paradox of pluralism

It has been frequently observed by scholars writing on the contemporary history of terrorism that the one-party states of the Communist World and the more powerful and ruthless military regimes of the Third World are the least troubled by challenges from terrorist movements. This is clearly mainly due to the fact that in such societies terror is the monopoly of the state: where the secret police are omnipotent it is hard to establish small islands of dissent and opposition to the regime.[14] This situation may well be changing in the USSR and other East European states now (1989) that *glasnost* is bringing greater pluralism and strident protest campaigns from the numerous ethnic minorities.[15]

It is indeed richly ironic that the first real signs of the emergence of genuine democratic freedoms in the communist states may well be the appearance of terrorist phenomena within those societies. Terrorism – a perversion of pluralism and democratic freedoms – may well be part of the price we pay for the relatively open and free societies of our liberal democratic world.

As regards the future of terrorism within liberal democratic societies, it is clear that it remains a serious threat to individual rights, and the wellbeing of whole communities, where the violence has become deeply entrenched – as for example in Northern Ireland and in Spain. In such societies citizens and governments clearly have a democratic duty to oppose and suppress the cancer of terrorism, while at the same time ensuring that this is done without destroying the rule of law and the democratic system.[16] This is by no means a simple task. However, we can gain some encouragement from the fact that Italy and West Germany have overcome quite vicious terrorist campaigns without destroying their own rights and liberties (see Lodge 1988; Langgath 1976; 1983; Drake 1984; Pisano 1985; Jamieson 1989).

A far more serious challenge faces the emerging democracies of the Third World. Countries such as India and Sri Lanka are experiencing far more acute levels of domestic terrorism than any Western industrial country has ever had. Yet they lack the economic and security resources to protect their populations adequately and suppress the terrorist violence swiftly and effectively. In such circumstances the temptation to suspend totally civil rights, due process of law and democratic government, in the name of the 'emergency', may become irresistible. Foreign powers are likely to seek to intervene, directly and through proxies, to exploit the opportunities for their own strategic purposes. In the worst circumstances what begins as a relatively small-scale terrorist campaign may lead to full-scale civil war, or even international war, with all the attendant dangers to regional peace and security.

V

Liberal democracy's resilience

Although it is demonstrably true that the growth of open liberal democratic societies increases the opportunities for terrorists to organize and initiate acts of violence, it is also clear that vigorous and effective democracies are particularly resilient in the face of terrorist efforts to overthrow them. Terrorist theoreticians know this full well. Feliks Gross (1969) points out that the antecedent conditions for terror against democracy are not only the existence of a terroristic organisation and leaders, but also erosion of shared democratic values, a state of anomie, or a crisis of democratic institutions. Invariably terror against democracy is preceded by a pre-assassination phase aimed at subverting and defaming democratic leaders and institutions.

Taking the longer-term view, two developments give grounds for greater optimism with regard to the future vulnerability of liberal democratic systems to terrorism.

First, ideological terrorism stemming from the extreme left has undoubtedly suffered a considerable decline in all the democracies where it was once quite well established – Italy, West Germany and Japan.[17] Even among the revolutionary student Left, the tactics and theory of terrorism have become discredited. It is true that there are tiny residues of the

Japanese Red Army, the Red Brigades and the Red Army Faction still at large. Some of them are living abroad. But although they may be capable of mounting an occasional outrage, they are politically a spent force. It is no longer 'radical chic' to get involved in terrorism. On the contrary, the terrorist movements' survivors have become regarded as a pathetic irrelevance, strangely out of touch with the real-life issues of social movements like the 'Greens' and the reviving socialist political parties (see Horchem 1987).

Second, the undermining of the support base of left-wing extremism has obviously been hastened by the crisis in the world's main communist regimes and parties. The massacre of the Chinese students campaigning for democracy has in the most tragic way brought home to young people in the West the brutality and moral and political bankruptcy of communism. And whereas the young Red Brigadists were angered and frustrated by what they saw as the 'treason' of the PCI in abandoning its commitment to revolutionary action, young people of the late 1980s applaud Gorbachev's efforts to liberalize the Soviet political and economic system, and see no appeal in the straitjacket of old-style communist ideology. In the long run the decline of Marxist–Leninist regimes and movements, worldwide, is bound to reduce the breeding ground for left-wing extremism and the terrorism it spawns.

This does not mean that the liberal democracies can afford to neglect other potential sources of extremist violence. The ultra right wing and anti-immigrant movements are an ugly force which, sadly, is still growing in certain countries and regions.[18] Far more worrying because on a much larger scale, we are witnessing the continuing growth of religious fanaticism and ethnic separation, both of which are notoriously prone to generate high levels of political violence.

VI

Conclusion

This brief paper has argued that terrorism is a deliberate policy for waging terror, usually for political ends; it is the systematic and calculated use of terrorization and is explicitly rationalized and justified by some philosophy, theory or ideology, however crude.

Almost invariably terrorists will claim that they use their violence only for the achievement of freedom. Certainly the growth of democratic political freedoms provides the terrorist movements with much greater opportunities to launch and conduct their campaigns of violence.

In ideological and political terms, however, terrorism is inherently incompatible with the values and institutions of liberal democracy; indeed, it systematically seeks to destroy them.

In view of this fundamental philosophical contradiction there is a pressing need to educate democratic societies, not only to assist them to uphold and strengthen the institutions and values of freedom and the rule of law, but also to recognize that terrorism is a totally illegitimate and morally unacceptable means of striving for a cause, especially within a liberal democratic society.

Terrorists are fond of using romantic euphemisms; they claim to be revolutionary heroes yet they commit cowardly acts, and lack the heroic qualities of humanity and magnanimity. They profess to be revolutionary soldiers yet they attack only by stealth, murder and maim the innocent, and disdain all rules and conventions of war. They claim to bring liberation when in reality they generally seek power for themselves.

Notes

1. For a classic exposition of the problems involved in the evaluative nature of the concepts used in the study of social behaviour, see Weber 1964: 88 ff.
2. This point has long been conceded by the mainstream thinkers in contemporary social science. See for example Berger 1963 and Runciman 1963.
3. For an examination of these underlying values see Wilkinson 1986: 1–68.
4. For an invaluable survey on the multiplicity of government response measures, see Friedlander 1978; 1979; 1981; 1984.
5. This view is forcibly expressed by J. Thackrah (1987a).
6. For a forceful presentation of this view, see Walzer 1973.
7. *Protocols additional to the Geneva Conventions of 12 August 1949.* International Committee of the Red Cross, Geneva, 1977, Articles 48–56.
8. This is not an idea peculiar to modern revolutionary terrorists. See John Most's denunciation of 'law and order' in *Freiheit*, 25 July 1885.
9. The PFLP's first communiqué, 11 December 1967, excerpted in *Arab World*, 12 December 1967.
10. *Tasks of the New Stage*, PFLP, Foreign Relations Committee, Beirut,1973.
11. In the 1989 local elections in Northern Ireland the support for the Provisional IRA's political wing, Provisional Sinn Fein, dropped to below 12 per cent of those voting.
12. See Wilson 1989 for an excellent analysis of this paradox.
13. This process is brilliantly observed in Confino 1974: 250 ff.
14. See Alexander 1976; Bassiouni 1974; Clutterbuck 1986; Gleason 1980; Goren 1984; Gutteridge 1986; Kupperman and Trent 1979; Laqueur 1987; *Patterns of Terrorism*, US Department of State, Washington DC, published annually, esp 1980–88.
15. For a masterly analysis of these trends, see Lieven 1989.
16. For a detailed discussion of the dilemmas involved, see Wilkinson 1986.

17.   See Lodge 1988; *Patterns of Terrorism*, op. cit. n.14.
18.   On these phenomena see Wilkinson 1983; *Committee of Inquiry into the Rise of Fascism and Racism in Europe: Report on the Findings*, European Parliament, Strasbourg, December 1985; von Beyme 1988.

4. Terrorists or Freedom Fighters

David George

I

Not everyone agreed with Lt.-Col. Oliver North's description of the Contras as Nicaraguan freedom fighters, among them the British Labour Party spokesman on foreign affairs, Gerald Kaufman. He said they were terrorists seeking to subvert the lawful government of Nicaragua. Their disagreement confirms a wellworn dictum – 'One man's terrorist is another man's freedom fighter' – as an empirical observation. Public opinion appears to be ambivalent toward the practice of political violence, a division which is reflected in popular usage. Ordinarily, 'freedom fighter' and 'terrorist' are used interchangeably, the terms having the same denotation, but opposite moral connotations. What one party sees as morally permissible, or even morally praiseworthy, and calls 'freedom fighting', an opposing party condemns as morally indefensible by labelling it 'terrorism'. What is, and what is not, terrorism, depends which side you are on.

These facts of ordinary usage are often taken to imply a radical moral relativism. The same actions of the same people can be both morally defensible 'freedom fighting' and morally indefensible 'terrorism', if moral judgments depend on, and are relative to, the diverse moral beliefs of the appraisers, or of the groups to which they belong. But if it is possible to use the words 'freedom fighting' and 'terrorism' to describe significantly different violent activities of different people in conjunction with their opposite moral connotations, the relativism is averted. One man's terrorist is then every man's terrorist, and no man's freedom fighter. To draw the required conceptual distinction between the two is the aim of this essay.

On the face of it, the problem is easily resolved: freedom fighters may be distinguished by the end they pursue, freedom, while terrorists can be defined by the means they employ, terror. 'Freedom fighter' and 'terrorist' cannot be interchangeable terms as it is possible to fight for freedom by

54

means other than terror and to employ terror in pursuit of other ends than freedom (Graham 1985: 44). A dichotomy of means and ends will not differentiate them completely though as it is consistent with freedom fighters resorting to terror, and terrorists pursuing freedom. However extensive this mixed category proves to be, it implies that one man's terrorist is only sometimes another man's freedom fighter, and *that* is enough to refute relativism, at least here.

II

Kill a chicken to frighten the monkey (Chinese Proverb)

Terrorism is the method or technique of instrumental terror, and terrorists are those who use it. On this view, a terrorist is someone who furthers his ends by perpetrating acts of extreme violence in order to terrorize people into compliance. He tries to extort gains either from the terrorized victim of his violent act, or, more usually, from a terrorized third party. In the tripartite version, victims are subjected to violence by the terrorist, not in order to terrorize them into altering their conduct to the advantage of the terrorist, but to send a terrible signal to an intended audience of this violence. The target of terror is this other party, simply because its attention, support, submission, or other response, alone is sought to serve terrorist ends. Terror is thus a necessary feature of terrorism; without it neither kind of terrorist extortion is possible. Terrorism simply *is* this abstract technique of extortion, a pure means unconnected to any particular end, or promiscuously available 'for an infinite variety of goals' (Wilkinson 1989: 12). This interpretation is, however, open to a double objection: acts of terrorism do not necessarily terrorize, and acts which do terrorize instrumentally need not be acts of terrorism. On both counts terrorists cannot be defined as those who employ terror as a means to their ends.

Many types of action terrorize instrumentally and yet are obviously not acts of terrorism. Common criminals, like those of the Mafia, whose extreme violence is extorsive, or the maniac with a gun who fires it at random targets, such as Michael Ryan at Hungerford, indubitably terrorize people in pursuit of their private purposes, yet do not count as terrorists. This is due partly to the private nature of their purposes, but where terror is instrumental to public ends, those responsible are not often counted as terrorists. Leaders of states armed with nuclear weapons who seek international peace through a balance of terror, Oriental despots (according to Montesquieu), Romans who followed the maxim *delenda est Carthago* in the final Punic war, RAF aircrew engaged in 'terror (area) bombing', were terrorizers not terrorists. To say that whoever terrorizes is *ipso facto* a terrorist is either an etymological confusion, or else an arbitrary stipulation of meaning. Instrumental terror is not a necessary and sufficient condition for an action to be terrorist. Whether its employment as a means is even a necessary condition of an act of terrorism must now be considered.

The second, and radical, part of the objection is sustained if terror is not an invariable feature of unambiguous acts of terrorism, because what is variable cannot be necessary. There are such acts which terrorize no one. They include expressivist bombings of buildings and similar properties (e.g. Nelson's column in Dublin) which are carried out because of their symbolic significance to the terrorist. Other attacks on property, say, propaganda by the deed to publicise and elicit support for the cause, are meant to arouse quite different feelings to those of terror which, from a terrorist's point of view, is counterproductive here. Indeed, it has been argued that any terrorist act intended to capture public attention succeeds only in so far as it breaks a social taboo in a novel, unexpected way, not by terrorizing its audience.[1] Instrumental terror is also absent when subjects of violence and extortion have no salient characteristic in common, that feature which indicates the likelihood of the latter becoming a victim in the event of noncompliance. The IRA's intention in murdering a builder who carried out work on police or military installations in Ulster is to deter all builders from undertaking similar work; to 'collaborate' is to become a 'legitimate target'. But a government will not become the victim of terrorists who have seized some of its citizens as hostages if it fails to meet their demands, which is why it is immune to terror. Terrorists therefore seek governments' compliance through the pressures of a public opinion excited by the taking and holding of hostages. Hunger strikes, like the IRA ones of 1981, are another example of terrorist extortion being attempted through an aroused public opinion, not through terror, for the moral blackmail of a government by self-inflicted violence terrorizes nobody. Finally, it may be noted that even where a target of terror is a prerequisite for a particular terrorist act, 'terror' in this context should not always be taken literally; it may also refer to lesser degrees of fear like anxiety, awe, apprehension, or intimidation (Freedman 1983: 399; Schmid 1988: 19–21).

The maxim on the lips of Chinese officials during June 1989, 'Kill one to teach one hundred', is not necessarily a terrorist precept then, because an instrumental use of terror is a contingent, albeit a common, characteristic of terrorism. A dichotomy of means and ends in which it is essential is not valid therefore, but it can be redrawn. In this new version, the method of terrorists is killing, or other severe harming, of innocent people.

III

Hostilities against the innocent

Terrorist attacks are often said to be acts of indiscriminate violence. By this is usually meant that they do not discriminate between illegitimate and legitimate targets of violence, or between the innocent and the guilty; not that they neglect to choose their targets on some criterion. Intentionally killing or seriously injuring innocent people is the distinctive method or the 'means' of terrorists, it is said (Walzer 1973: 198; Primoratz 1989). Freedom fighters, by contrast, are supposedly selective in their violence; unlike the terrorists, they have no victims, because their attacks are confined to the not-innocent. Terrorists are distinguished from freedom fighters by the difference in their targets, then, a difference which accounts for the morally indefensible character of terrorism, and the moral permissibility of freedom fighting. A line dividing legitimate from illegitimate targets can be drawn in more than one way, but it is usually drawn as a distinction between combatants and noncombatants (see, for example, Coady 1985: 52–65).

Combatants are members of a belligerent power who have a certain public status through direct participation in war by fighting; noncombatants are those excluded from this status, either by nonparticipation in the public activity of war, or by participating in another, indirect, way. Combatants are not legitimate targets on account of shared guilt, however, and if they were, hardly any could rightfully be killed, wounded or taken prisoner; only those of them who had knowingly and voluntarily engaged in unjust war (Teichman 1986: 57–8, 63–4). Combatants are legitimate targets only in, and because of, war; through them the war is waged by belligerent parties: of necessity, hostilities are directed against them. As armed agents of a belligerent, they attack enemy combatants to disable them from further fighting, and they defend against such disabling attacks on themselves, always with a view to overpowering an adverse belligerent power. In so far as war is itself a legitimate activity, they are legitimate targets to enemy combatants. Noncombatants can never be such targets, regardless of their innocence, or lack of it, simply because they are not the armed forces of a belligerent through whom it wages war.

Both can be attacked, but only within a war, and then only by another combatant. A noncombatant *qua* noncombatant cannot attack anyone, but in his private capacity that same individual can (unlawfully) attack anybody else, not as combatants or as noncombatants, but solely in their private capacity. If terrorists or freedom fighters resort to arms as noncombatants, they do not wage legitimate acts of war, but simply violate the Law of War. The war crimes they commit are the same, whether the victim was a serviceman or a civilian (both could be noncombatants or combatants in their public wartime capacity), for neither is a legitimate target. And where legitimate targets do not exist, freedom fighters are indistinguishable from terrorists. Groups like the IRA, the PLO, the Red Brigades, or the ANC, operate in peacetime, however, so there are no combatants (and hence no noncombatants) to attack. Any civilian or serviceman they kill, wound or take captive, is thereby an innocent victim of a morally outrageous crime.

Against this, members of the groups may say that peace is an illusion; that class war, race war, or some similar war is the reality; and that from time to time the war erupts in fighting between class (or other) combatants. Usually though, they are self-styled combatants in a war they claim to have begun by taking up arms against a supposed enemy. Whichever it is, *they* determine unilaterally the belligerent parties and decide the legitimate targets, regardless of the judgement of others and without reference to the Law of War. Decisions taken are ideologically informed instead. If they are right, freedom fighters and terrorists are, in principle, distinguishable, because there are combatant and noncombatant targets. But given the identity of those determining who are combatants, this is highly unlikely in practice. Intended targets will inevitably be defined as legitimate targets, otherwise attacks on people previously stated to be illegitimate targets will have to be acknowledged. No one will be a terrorist when everyone is a 'combatant' who only attacks 'enemy combatants'. On the other hand, if the situation is not one of war, they will lack the status of combatants, and be private individuals taking up arms to commit common crime (and thus be indistinguishable).

Of the two, the second alternative is more probable. Groups like the ones listed above are not corporate public entities with a right of war (as were the American colonies in 1775). Rather, they are simply collections of private individuals whose private acts of violence are mere crimes, no matter against whom they are directed, just as piracy or banditry are not small-scale warfare. Moreover, they set no limits and tolerate no imposed restraints upon their violence; everything is permitted to those whose sole criterion of conduct is the necessity of the 'cause'. Terrorism, not war, is hell. War is a rule governed activity (Clark 1988: 24–9), in which the primary function of the externally imposed rules is limitation of war's violence. As the Hague Regulations on Land Warfare state: 'The right of belligerents to adopt means of injuring the enemy is not unlimited'. Whether terrorism is, or is not, war, it cannot be the method of attacking innocent noncombatants. In a war in which they were supposed combatants, terrorists would be systematically committing war crimes, not engaging in combat, were they to employ this method. However, if they are noncombatants, they are incapable of attacking either combatants or noncombatants since they act as private individuals. And the distinction between the two is inapplicable in peacetime.

Since combatants and noncombatants, in general, are equally innocent from a legal or a moral point of view, guilt and innocence have so far played no part in distinguishing legitimate from illegitimate targets. But in another version of the distinction, both are of decisive importance. Michael Walzer (1973: 198) defines terrorism as 'the random murder of innocent people', of citizens and noncombatant civilians. Noncombatant immunity from attack is due to military innocence, he argues; civilians bear no arms to threaten, or harm, anyone. Similarly, citizens are innocent politically; they harm no one for, unlike officials, they are never agents of unjust, oppressive regimes. Some officials are legitimate targets then, but all other citizens deserve an equivalent immunity to noncombatants. Walzer claims this is provided by a code of honour among revolutionaries, the counterpart to the war convention which limits targets to combatants.[2] At this point, however, the parallel breaks down.

Officials like soldiers, are agents of a state (the citizen body). Agents act on behalf of a principal, pursue his purposes, using powers given to them by him. Provided they do not act *ultra vires,* agents must be innocent if their principal is innocent and guilty if he is not. So if officials are legitimate targets, citizens must be too. Or, if a state is a belligerent, it merits attack just as much as its agents, the combatants. The principle of noncombatant immunity prohibits such attacks, but this principle is just a conventional (hence, inessential) rule of war, albeit one based upon a longstanding consensus among belligerent powers. A similarly comprehensive agreement giving immunity to citizens, while allowing officials to be the legitimate objects of revolutionary violence, does not exist. There is just the code of honour and it is a unilateral convention; only in the eyes of (some) revolutionaries are some public officials exclusively the legitimate targets. Even then, self-imposed limits may be lifted as easily as imposed. Revolution, in short, is not a rule-governed activity like war, and that is why officials are not the counterparts of combatants or citizens the double of noncombatants. Thus, for example, if it were the case that the British government is responsible for unjust laws, or other oppressions, in Ulster, the IRA-attempted assassination of its leading members at a Brighton hotel in 1984 was still not an act of revolutionary freedom fighting, but one of terrorism.

Terrorism is not the method of attacking innocent people such as Walzer's citizens or other illegitimate targets like noncombatants for these several reasons. A further consideration is that the instrumentality of this method is dubious. For example, how a massacre of Puerto Rican Christian pilgrims to the Holy Land and other passengers at Lod Airport in 1972 was supposed to serve the end of 'liberating Palestine' is obscure. The statement after the event by the Popular Front for the Liberation of Palestine, ' There are no innocent tourists in Israel', was meant to excuse, not explain it. Many random attacks on innocent people do not appear to be self-sufficient means to terrorists' ends, but (supposedly) an effective way of terrorizing them, in which case it is terror that is directly instrumental and indiscriminate attacks only indirectly so. But terror is inessential to terrorism, it was argued earlier, and given that this is the case, it must be true of a means to terror too, namely, hostilities against the innocent .

So far, then, it has proved impossible to distinguish terrorists by the means they employ. The one indubitably essential feature of terrorist methods – extreme, usually lethal, violence – is anything but unique to terrorism. However, there is at least a prospect of success in trying to differentiate freedom fighters by the end they pursue: freedom.

IV

Armed struggle for freedom

Freedom fighters are widely regarded as those who pursue the liberation of a people from foreign rule and domination (national self-determination) *vi et armis*.[3] This end supposedly legitimates all violent means, no matter how atrocious (UN General Assembly Resolution 3103/XXVII), in addition to differentiating them from terrorism. Two years after Israeli athletes were murdered by his gunmen at the Munich Olympics, Yasser Arafat made this point in a widely applauded speech to the UN General Assembly: 'He who fights for a just cause, he who fights for the liberation of his country, he who fights against invasion and exploitation or single-mindedly against colonialism, can never be defined as a terrorist'. Terrorists fought against just causes or waged war to occupy, colonize or oppress other peoples, he added (Arafat 1986: para. 48).

Terrorists, with the possible exception of those who profess to be waging a jihad,[4] also represent their activities as the liberation of an oppressed group from its oppression by an armed struggle against the oppressor. Freedom is their supreme end too and in the same sense of the word, namely, independence or autonomy of a group. The only significant difference arises over the identity of the oppressed group which is the intended beneficiary of their emancipatory activities: the proletariat, *la peuple-classe*, unborn babies, peoples or nations, the Aryan race, *les damnés de la terre*, animals, and so on. This implies that defining the liberation of one such group as freedom fighting and that of the remainder as terrorism is a wholly arbitrary discrimination. Any alternative stipulation is equally valid and, indeed, this is why 'freedom fighter' and 'terrorist' are interchangeable terms in ordinary usage. 'Freedom fighters' are those with a just cause, 'terrorists' those without one (who may, in addition, oppose a just cause), and every terrorist is someone's freedom fighter.

In rebuttal, it may be said that significant differences occur over what counts as freedom-as-autonomy. Autonomy, in the present context, can mean anything from the future communist society to animals released from cages, and often there is a considerable overlap in its meanings. In the case of national liberation, its primary meaning is political independence or self-government, but there are additional economic, social and cultural dimensions to its signification (*UN Declaration Concerning Friendly Relations*, 1970). These secondary aspects are vague and indeterminate and many Third World countries have interpreted them so that the pursuit of national liberation (especially after political independence) amounts to one form or another of an anti-imperialist socialism, not excluding its Marxist variants (MacFarlane 1985: ch. 4). But even the primary aspect of the nationalist goal is a sufficiently imprecise and elastic concept to permit virtually any group attempting to overthrow its own government to profess it as their end. Both Sandinistas and Contras at different times have claimed their own attempt to topple the current government in Managua was armed struggle for national liberation, in the one case from US domination, in the other from the Soviet sway. It must be allowed there are important differences in the character of the autonomy of oppressed groups then, but far from contributing to the distinction needed they seem to blur differences. As a final reply it might be suggested that the end being pursued differs from the ostensible one of freedom, except in the case of national liberation; that the emancipation of the proletariat, say, is really an imposition of totalitarian communist tyranny. It seems safe to conclude that armed struggle for such causes is terrorism, not fighting for freedom. National self-determination, however, is vulnerable to exactly the same objection; that the 'liberated' nation is simply one subject to a native, rather than a foreign, despotism. Thus, far from solving the problem of demarcation, nothing more significant has been achieved than relocating the previous relativism. Now it takes the form, 'One man's freedom is another man's slavery.' No objective demarcation can be based on acceptance of that proposition.

It is finally time to abandon the attempt to distinguish freedom fighters from terrorists by a means/end dichotomy, in which both means and ends have been examined in their usual interpretations. Terrorists characteristically, though not necessarily, terrorize people in pursuit of their ends. And if they necessarily attack the innocent, no satisfactory way of distinguishing them from freedom fighters, in this respect, was found. As for the pursuit of freedom as the *summum bonum* in politics, only an arbitrary restriction of its application to nations separated freedom fighters from terrorists. The most the dichotomy offered was a partial distinction between freedom fighters and terrorists, rather than their mutual exclusivity, but not even that was achieved. Some pointers to what is required in a reasonably well drawn distinction have nonetheless been uncovered. In the first place, the violence of the freedom fighter will be restricted to non-innocent targets and limited to attaining the end of freedom, whereas terrorists flout both principles. In general, freedom fighting will be a rule-governed activity; terrorism, a ruleless activism. Second, freedom fighting will be for a just cause, freedom, but it will be civil liberty not the absolute freedom of group autonomy sought through armed struggle. Third, these differences will coincide with the moral connotations of the words, 'terrorist' and 'freedom fighter'. In sum, the distinction between the two is the difference between (just) armed resistance and (unjust) armed struggle. Its nature will now be outlined.

V

Armed resistance

To begin, it will be helpful to consider the paradigm of armed resistance, the Partisans or Maquis who fought against the Nazi occupation of their country during the Second World War. In a few cases, towards the end of the war, resistance movements were made part of a belligerent's armed forces, but mostly they operated as irregular forces on their own initiative, with no authorization. They were no ordinary groups of civilians, however. Under the Hague Regulations (1907), they achieved combatant status, enjoying the same privileges as members of a belligerent's armed forces. Provided they carried their arms openly, wore a fixed emblem recognizable at a distance, were commanded by persons responsible for their subordinates and operated according to the laws and customs of war, they could not be treated as war criminals when they engaged in acts of sabotage, armed attacks on troops and other similarly violent, clandestine and sporadic operations against enemy occupying forces. Their legal right under positive international law may have been secure, but did they have a corresponding moral right?

Belligerent occupation of a country, as such, is a lawful act; as much as any other act of war it is legitimate. Armed resistance to an occupation is therefore a conflict of (legal) rights. It will also be manifestly just if the occupying power abuses its lawful military power over the territory and its inhabitants, by systematically violating the Laws of War applicable to belligerent occupation. If instead of administering a country according to existing laws, ensuring public order and safety and respecting human rights to life, property, religious and other liberties, an occupying power seizes and exploits private and public property in the interests of its own war effort, deports inhabitants to use as slave labour, exterminates large sections of the population in addition to perpetrating outright genocide, subjects inhabitants to random, indiscriminate acts of violence (like those resulting from implementation of the 1941 decrees, Barbarossa and *Nacht und Nebel*) in order to terrorize them into submission, the administration is no longer a lawful occupant. It is a lawless regime which has systematically and violently attacked the inhabitants in a series of major war crimes, an extreme example of tyranny *ab exercito*. Thus the moral right of the wartime Resistance was the right of self-defence against the tyrannical aggression of Nazi rule.

Its just cause was to exercise this right in the only way possible, by overthrowing (or rather, assisting in the overthrow of) the tyrant, through force of arms; that is, to liberate the native land from the lawless regime. However, if the liberation was intended as a prelude to imposing another, civilian, form of tyranny – communism, say – it would be perverse to treat members of the Resistance movement concerned as freedom fighters, especially when they try to eliminate other resistance groups whose aim is to restore constitutional government in the postwar world. Constitutional government takes many forms, but in each the cardinal feature is the rule of law and it is this which makes it the direct opposite of tyranny. Strictly, tyranny is an exercise of a claim to subject people to the absolute and arbitrary power of the claimant; to do with them as he pleases, without restriction and for his exclusive benefit. This is tantamount to claiming a right to enslave, for not only is personal liberty denied; all rights are rejected. It is therefore the most fundamental assault possible upon a human being. This was exactly the regime against which members of the Resistance in occupied Europe fought, according to its leading historian, M.R.D. Foot. He writes: 'Resisters were prepared to assert the rule of law against a regime that derided it … . They saw Nazis treating men and women like cattle and were quite sure this would not do' (Foot 1978: 6). The eradication of this tyranny is an act of liberation, but freedom is not secured until the establishment of a rule of law and constitutional government. The former is the necessary and sufficient condition of liberty in its fundamental form, freedom from the arbitrary restraints and violence of others including (especially) that of governments. Constitutional government is the antithesis of tyranny in that its powers are subject to, and limited by, law. Under the law a person is not subject to the arbitrary will of another, observed Locke (1956: *Second Treatise*, para. 57), but freely follows his own. This condition, 'civil liberty', was the goal of the Resistance (in general) and why they were freedom fighters in the fullest sense of the word.

It was pursued by armed force against the occupation forces, not all of whom were morally responsible for the evils of the regime. But Resistance members had two rights to exercise: a legal one to attack enemy combatants, regardless of their moral status, and a moral right of self-defence against the lawless Nazi regime of occupation, a right not limited to its military agents. Exercising these rights did not violate the Just War principle that prohibits attacks on innocent noncombatants; the violence was discriminate. It is also arguable that the means employed were proportionate to the ends they adopted, both in the sense that an economy of force was employed and in the means being compatible with the end pursued. Means and ends of the Resistance were interconnected, both being grounded in law and limits.

This is to make the further point that freedom fighting, as exemplified by the Resistance, is a concrete activity, not an opposite abstraction to that of terrorism (as a 'means').[5] If it is a misconception to think of terrorism as an all-purpose technique serving no end, or no kind of end, in particular, and this was the burden of the argument earlier, it is no less mistaken to take freedom fighting as the pursuit of freedom in any sense of the term and in any way bar one, terror. In summary, its violent methods are rule-governed, discriminate and, at least in some senses, proportionate to its end of eradicating the lawless, liberty-denying, regime of tyranny and replacing it by the rule of law and a constitutional government where civil liberty is enjoyed. Freedom fighting, in this sense, is a relatively uncommon phenomenon; its range extends to rebellions such as the eighteenth-century one by the thirteen American colonies and to tyrannicides like the plot to assassinate Hitler in July 1944, but no further.[6] Terrorism, as a concrete activity or unity of means and ends, is its antithesis, that is, it is a tyranny in the name of freedom.

VI

The tyranny of terrorism

If the essential claim of the freedom fighter was the right of self-defence against the radical assault of tyranny, the essential one of the terrorist is an unlimited right of attack upon anyone. It is expressly articulated from time to time, as, for example, by George Habash, leader of the PFLP, who said, 'in today's world, no one is innocent and no one is neutral' (Hayes 1980: 9), or earlier, in 1894, by the French anarchist terrorist, Emile Henry. After his arrest following the bombing of a Parisian café crowded with clerks, shopkeepers and workers, he was reproached for taking innocent lives. His response was: '*Il n'y a pas d'innocents*' (Salmon 1959: 343). When no one is innocent or rather, no one is regarded as innocent, everyone becomes a legitimate target to the terrorist; his violence is wholly and necessarily indiscriminate. Any particular victim or victims selected could always have been somebody else; the choice is invariably unpredictable, unavoidable, and entirely arbitrary. What is claimed therefore is a universal and absolute right; universal because it is against all people, absolute because it is a right to do with them as he sees fit, unrestricted by law, human rights or any other moral considerations. It is, in short, the lawless right of tyranny to kill, to take captive, to rob and to terrorize at will.

Terrorism is the exercise of this 'right' of tyranny, though terrorists differ from earlier tyrants in one crucial respect. A tyrant was thought to rule for his personal gratification or benefit; the terrorist exercises his claim against everyone in the name of a public good: freedom. But it is a freedom in keeping with the boundless nature of his violence, limitless or 'absolute' freedom (see Hegel 1910: 592–605), the freedom-as-autonomy sought by participants in armed struggle. A group, like a nation or social class, is fully free or autonomous only in so far as it completely governs itself or directs its own affairs. Unless all its circumstances are the product of its will, it is not self-determined but other-directed. Whatever acts as a barrier or is otherwise an obstacle to its free exercise must be swept away as heteronomous and oppressive, not excluding its own previous volitions. Anything not founded on the will of the group is devoid of legitimacy and a candidate for elimination at the earliest opportunity. Thus the quest for absolute freedom is an endless striving to refashion the world to conform with the prescriptions of the (rational) will of the proletariat, the Aryan race, the Palestinian people or some such group. It presupposes current imperfections, in particular the miseries of present 'oppression', are not God-given, natural or, in some other way, intrinsic: that all are the outcome of a radically defective, but changeable, organization of society that has been created and maintained by an oppressive, exploitative countergroup, the 'enemy of the people' (for example, the bourgeoisie, *das Gegenvolk* and the Zionist entity). In all this, the self-appointed, though not single-handed, task of the terrorist is to deliver the nation, class, race and so on from its present tribulations of heteronomy, variously called 'capitalism', 'Zionism', 'colonialism' or 'neocolonialism', 'NATO imperialism', 'US imperialism', and the rest, by enlisting in a secret 'army' against the people's enemy ('representatives' of one or other of these multifarious forms of heteronomy) to engage it in armed struggle. Needless to say, this enterprise of liberation is far removed from the pursuit of civil liberty and constitutional government by fighting for the overthrow of the lawless, tyrannical, in fact, terrorist, regime that was the Nazi Third Reich.

VII

Review and conclusion

It may prove impossible to prevent 'terrorist' and 'freedom fighter' from being used interchangeably in common parlance, but this essay has not been an exercise in linguistic reform. Nor has it attempted to provide a full account of either freedom fighting or its opposite, terrorism, though it is preparative to such an account. As it stands, it is an essay in conceptual analysis, in definition and demarcation, only. Its aim was to deny a claim of J. L. Mackie: ' Notoriously, the same people and the same activities look very different from opposing points of view. What one party sees as terrorist gunmen, another sees as fearless freedom fighters' (1977: 238), and the moral relativism it seemed to imply. It succeeds to the extent that terrorism can be accurately described as a tyrannical activity and freedom fighting as its negation. And if it fails, then at least a tolerably coherent case has been made that terrorism and freedom fighting are not a pair of opposite abstractions: a means that is independent of all ends and an end which has no relation to any means in particular except the one it excludes.

Notes

1. Crenshaw-Hutchinson (1972: 385) argues that audiences not directly threatened by terrorists experience curiosity, sympathy and even admiration for them. See also Crenshaw 1986: 401–2.
2. In addition to Walzer's examples of the code (1973: 198–9), see Iviansky 1986: 74–7, and Nedava 1986: 60–62.
3. Thackrah 1987b: 87. Admittedly, this is a narrower concept than fighting for freedom by means other than terror, but 'other means' includes words. We do not normally think of those who fight for freedom in this fashion as freedom fighters and if we did no one would confuse them with terrorists. See Bell 1944, Barnard 1971 and Philp 1987.
4. This would not be true of that Lebanese group which styles itself the *Islamic Jihad for the Liberation of Palestine*.
5. This point is recognized, to a limited extent, by McGurn 1987: 53.
6. For justification of this claim in respect of tyrannicide and an indication of its application to rebellion, see George 1988: 390–419.

5. Terrorism: Historical Roots and Moral Justifications

Robert Phillips

I

When nations find themselves in trouble, it is usually the case that their difficulties are a long time in the making. The current wave of terrorism washing over the nations of the West has an intellectual history, one which turns out to be rather unflattering to those who see themselves as the main victims of these new developments.

Three large philosophical ideas have steadily gained strength over the past two hundred years and now appear on the stage of history in the form of violent and indiscriminate attacks upon innocent people. Ironically, these ideas are all peculiarly Western in that they presuppose both the Western tradition of political and ethical theory as well as Western technology.

The ideas are: popular sovereignty, the principle of self-determination, and ethical consequentialism. Before looking at these in detail and showing their connection with modern terrorism, it is necessary to define terrorism. This task is not really difficult: terrorism is the direct attack upon innocent people with the intention of radically altering some political or social situation. By means of such attacks, the terrorists hope to detach the loyalty of a population from its government by demonstrating that their government cannot perform its end of the social contract – it cannot protect the lives, liberties, and property of its citizens. Never mind that no democratic government has been destabilized by these tactics; terrorists act out of a sense of desperation and they will keep trying. I suggest that such difficulties as academics, journalists and politicians have had in getting a handle on terrorism arise not because of any difficulty in defining the phenomenon, but in trying to define it in such a way that terrorism will be an appropriate description of the activities of our opponents but not of our own. This is ultimately self-defeating and will be seen by neutral observers as hypocrisy. Moral denunciations of terrorism are appropriate and mandatory. Terrorist acts are profoundly immoral and, in addition, tend not to be the short cut which their practitioners advertise. One has only to look at the areas of the world where terror has held sway to see that violence is typically prolonged, sometimes indefinitely. The reason for this is not difficult to discern. Each side comes to perceive the other as 'criminal' and thus as beyond the pale of civilized negotiation.

While the Reagan administration was quite correct in its condemnation of terrorism as a means of effecting political and social change, such denunciations only make sense against a moral backdrop which (1) rigidly distinguishes between combatants and noncombatants and (2) equally rigidly adheres to the principle that innocent people have an absolute right not to be murdered for any reason whatever. Now it should be obvious that both of these tenets have been steadily eroding since 1940, as much in the West as elsewhere. Despite repeated commitments to a plethora of declarations of human rights, few, if any, governments are terribly scrupulous in their military policies regarding such rights. In what follows, I shall try to show how we got ourselves into this predicament.

II

Historical roots

The doctrine of popular sovereignty developed over the long haul of Western history as the profoundly moral idea that human beings are born free and equal and, as such, have a right to an equal share of political power. The slogan 'one man, one vote' perfectly expresses the idea that democracy is the fairest of all political decision procedures because it correctly reflects the human condition of natural freedom and equality. But almost from the beginning it was observed that popular sovereignty also tends to diffuse responsibility for political acts, particularly acts of war. It is now a commonplace that everything from conscription to the saturation bombing of civilian centres in the Second World War traces its rationale to popular sovereignty. If the people are the state, then is it not their responsibility both to defend the state and to bear the burden of attacks upon it? This question has never been satisfactorily answered. Despite efforts in international law to distinguish between degrees of culpability with regard to politicians, generals, and ordinary citizens, policies of direct attacks upon civilians continue to find a rationale in the identification of the citizen with the state. And this is so even if the ordinary citizen is both ignorant of and indifferent to affairs of state. For the principle of popular sovereignty, enshrined in the US constitution, has provided modern states with the moral leverage to nationalize the lives of its citizens in a way that puts them at risk. Terrorists of all stripes merely key into this idea and construe it to their own purposes. They are thus able to create much of the moral ambivalence expressed in 'One man's terrorist is another man's freedom fighter'.

The principle of self-determination is one of those nineteenth-century liberal ideas which gradually worked its way into the primary documents of the twentieth-century international law, including the UN Charter. The principle is, as such, well intentioned. It says that 'a people' have the right to determine the shape of their own lives and the disposition of the land upon which they live without the intervention of outside parties. Self-determination really came to the fore after 1945 as a rubric for decolonization at the time of the winding down of the old European empires. But gradually self-determination became synonymous with the right of every religious and ethnic group to have its own state. Despite the fact that demographics makes such a world unfeasible, terrorist groups continue to fly the banner of self-determination. They are able to get away with this because the principle is fatally flawed by vagueness. To give a single but crucial example: Ireland. During the long and bitter struggle in Northern Ireland, the Protestant Loyalists have steadfastly appealed to self-determination on the grounds that as 'a people' they have a right to shape their own future, which means, for them, continued membership in the UK. Catholic Nationalists appeal to the same principle with equal sincerity. For them self-determination means what 'the people' of the whole island of Ireland want. Thus, crucial to making self-determination work is the ability to specify which sample of a given population is to 'count' in 'What finally counts is what the people living there want'. Unfortunately, the principle of self-determination is silent on this point. The terrorist is not really playing fast and loose when he appeals to the principle of self-determination. It is the principle itself which is fast and loose. The idea of self-determination will continue to complicate efforts to deal with terrorism.

Ethical consequentialism also has a significant history. The moral tradition which shaped the West is an amalgam of Classical and Christian sources. This ethical unity is possible, despite considerable cultural diversity between the two sources, because in the end they are both agreed that the good life involves strict adherence to categorical moral principles. This bedrock underlies the soil of Western culture. To look first at the Classical source, both Plato and Aristotle were insistent that injustice was not permitted as a means to satisfying some project for the production of good consequences. In the *Republic* Plato makes this point in many diverse and intellectually subtle ways. He (like Aristotle) argues that there are certain basic human values which are simply worth having for their own sake and that the real 'consequence' of immoral behaviour is self-destruction. Plato, in one of the most powerful passages in Western philosophy, describes the decline of the unjust man into the tyrant, the most unhappy of all men. The main thrust of these classical arguments, then, is that the man of good character is also the only truly happy man. Maintaining such a character will involve avoiding injustice and, in particular, the pitfall of thinking it possible to do evil that good may come of it. Plato was quite realistic about this matter, and he understood that such a life is difficult to achieve. And he was certainly extremely pessimistic about the possibility of the masses ever becoming just – the best they could hope for would be to live in a society governed by a just ruler. Nevertheless, he insists that there are objectively discernible goods, the participation in which constitutes the good life, and that such a life is irretrievably damaged by acts of injustice, undertaken even for the 'best' of reasons.

We have with Plato and Aristotle the beginnings of what was later to be called Natural Law. Central to Natural Law thinking is the Platonic insight that it is possible to define objectively what it means to be good at being a person; that just as there are standards of excellence for being a doctor and a teacher, so there are knowable standards of excellence for being human. By the same token the good society is one in which people are allowed to conform to these standards.

Consonant with these Classical insights, is the Judeao-Christian idea of a transcendent source of all value. God is both personal and creative, thus conferring immeasurable value upon human life. The commandments which govern the life of the Jew and the Christian are strictly categorical in nature, as indeed are most ethical codes which are based upon theistic sources. Friendship with God was firmly tied to carefully walking the path of justice, for it was understood that to damage any basic human value was to attack, to that extent, the very source of value and being. What Plato understood to be the real consequence of injustice – self-destruction – the Judeao-Christian tradition expands to include a cutting off of the very source of our being.

The absolutist conception of justice is reflected in the medieval tradition of Just War thinking, particularly in that aspect dealing with *jus in bello*. The notion that in war noncombatants must never be made the object of direct attacks is but one instance of the application of the categorical prohibition of murder to the realm of war. As these provisions of the Just War tradition passed into the newly developing corpus of international law in the seventeenth century, they retained their categorical or absolutist character. And, needless to say, the Christian churches continued to promulgate a similar view of justice, although now arguing from a much weakened position.

The foregoing mainstream tradition in ethics was, starting in the sixteenth century, subject to the beginning of a challenge which culminates in the nineteenth with the development and popularization of a full-blown consequentialism. Machiavelli is a key figure in this new tradition. He argued that while the Prince should adhere to the good, there will arise situations when state necessity will require the Prince to damage a known good in order to 'save the state'. The ends, that is, may justify evil means. Machiavelli is not entirely clear why the preservation of the political order outweighs any other known good, but we may understand his thinking as a response to the newly developing form of the centralized modern state. For by the sixteenth century, political states with their bureaucracies and centralized authority were recognizably 'modern'. In a world of absolute sovereign states, no structure exists to which appeal can be made over the heads of the princes. The state, therefore, becomes the only hope for the survival of any conception of the good life. As a transitional figure, Machiavelli reflects the tension between the new and the old ways of thinking about justice. On the one hand, he recognizes the good in a traditional sense – there are certain qualities of character that are worth having for their own sakes; goods which are self-evident in the sense that no argument or further justification is necessary for them. But, on the other hand, state necessity will require the sacrifice of some of these principles (in particular, the prohibition against murder) for a greater good. In the Prince we begin to see the outline of a certain type of modern man. First, he rejects the Classical warning that acting against the good will irretrievably damage one's own character in such a way that one will gradually lose altogether a knowledge of the good. The Prince, according to Machiavelli, is fundamentally unaffected by this. He is a technician in statecraft and, to that extent, beyond good and evil in the conventional sense. Second, he rejects the Christian notion of Divine Providence. The Prince must make his own future even where this involves doing evil. It is the Prince who plays God here in order to secure the desired outcome. And, of course, all of this is 'tragically necessary'.

What Machiavelli marks in the sixteenth century is finally brought to completion in the nineteenth by such philosophical giants as Bentham and

Mill, whose work clearly faced up to the pure consequentialism of much modern politics.

In its mature nineteenth century formulations, consequentialism was a theory devised, in part, to deal with the perceived problem of the supposed disappearance of generally agreed upon moral standards. The scepticism brought on in some quarters by the rise of empiricism, Darwinism, and various forms of atheism led to the search for some standard which would unite what appeared to be radically heterogeneous values. Mill and others, therefore, fixed upon certain subjective ends, styled variously as 'happiness' or 'pleasure'. Additionally, as the aforementioned belief in Divine Providence continued to decline, the terrible burden of completely securing the future seemed to fall entirely upon human shoulders, thus seeming, in principle, to rule out no possible course of action as wrong or absolutely impermissible in itself – no conceivable sacrifice of known goods as too great to secure the future. Moral rules thus lost their categorical force in the search for a means of maximizing the good over some set of future times. Thus moral rules are seen as breakable in principle when we calculate that such deviance will maximize the good or produce net beneficial consequences. Given the pervasiveness of this moral theory and its impact upon the common man, it is no accident that our own century is replete with political movements which require or threaten destruction of known values as a means of effecting a future of unlimited happiness.

It is worth reminding ourselves at this point that the belief in the mutability of moral obligations is one of the main strengths of the terrorist argument. For if there are no absolute human rights then the innocent will be, to that degree, in danger. 'Calculations' about whether or not to kill an innocent person are at bottom no more than arguments of pure advocacy. If the disputants are prepared to use a sufficiently long time-span during which the life prospects of the proposed victims can be charted, then it can be made to seem just as 'reasonable' not to kill them. But can we reasonably be expected to deal with other people on the basis of deciding whether they live or die by trying to project their life prospects over an indeterminate time period?

The diffusion of political responsibility, the belief that every group has a right to its own state, and the decline in the belief in absolute human rights, come together in our time to provide the intellectual climate for terrorism as well as for the moral ambivalence which many people feel when faced with acts of terror.

It is clear that terrorists the world over have simply appropriated concepts and episodes (Hiroshima, Dresden) generated in the West. But it should be equally clear that this fact should not in any way debilitate us in our fight against terrorism, a struggle which will be long, sad and bloody. No government, no matter what its own past transgressions, can fail to protect its own citizens. However, if anything positive can be said about this grim situation, it is that as victims of terrorism we may be forced to rethink our own policies on the use of force (including nuclear force) in order to bring them into line with our moral denunciations of terror. If such re-evaluation does occur then perhaps some good will emerge from this terrible evil.

III

Moral justifications

Given this historical and ideological background, we may now turn to an examination of arguments offered in moral justification of terrorism. There are essentially two lines of defence advanced by supporters of terrorism. First, as the basis for moral rejection of terrorism is the claim that there are noncombatants, people who have no direct connection with the military, apologists for terrorism have frequently sought to undermine the combatant/noncombatant distinction. They will argue that in today's world no one is neutral and no one is innocent. Thus, the PLO may kill Jewish children because they will grow up to be Jewish adults; they may kill the aged and the infirm because they are 'Zionists'. I have previously shown how the doctrine of popular sovereignty complicates efforts to answer this argument. Even so, it is obviously unreasonable to equate 'support' for a cause with the kind of militancy that would justify armed attack. In the context of international law as well as the Just War tradition force may be used as a last resort and when I am faced with an imminent threat to my life and rights. It is impossible to justify the killing of a child on these grounds. What Just War theory attempts here is to capture our moral intuition that in matters of force we ought to pay attention to what people are doing to us, or threatening to do. Only then are we treating them as fellow humans and not as a mere means to our own political and ideological purposes. Additionally, Just War theory has recognized a strong prudential strain in this matter. A world in which the distinction between combatants and noncombatants was erased would be a much more dangerous place. The escalation of violence attendant upon removing this distinction would be counterproductive, probably negating the political usefulness of the initial act of force.

Anyone who has seen the faces of civilians caught in the coils of the many wars of our century cannot but reject the terrorist's efforts to categorize them as 'combatants'. They are victims of what is to them usually a completely meaningless cataclysm equivalent to a natural disaster. This description is accurate even if they in a general way 'support' their government. For given the power and technological means available to modern states, we cannot but expect the average person to support the political order of which he is a member. In any event, the terrorist argument on this matter is usually applied with complete hypocrisy. When their terrorist camps in Lebanon are raided and civilians are inadvertently killed or when US jets bomb terrorist installations in Libya causing civilian damage, the terrorists decry this as cold-blooded murder. One cannot have it both ways – either there is a distinction between legitimate targets or there is not. In condemning those who kill their own women and children, they are tacitly admitting that the distinction does obtain.

A second attempt at moral justification finds the terrorist claiming that his activities are actually more humane than conventional warfare because terrorism constitutes a short cut. By directly attacking innocent people, the terrorist attempts to detach the loyalty of the populace from their government. When that happens the government will be forced to make concessions to the terrorists. So by a judicious use of terror (kill one, frighten a hundred) political change can be effected on the cheap. Although this is the terrorist advertisement, not a single modern state with even a shred of popular support has come close to being destabilized. Terrorists have certainly scored a number of triumphs, not the least of which is economic damage, but they have failed again and again over the past two decades to destabilize any state either by turning its citizens against it or by forcing the state into a repressive mode. Thus, the much vaunted moral argument of a short cut has no historical instances.

The reasons for the failure of the short cut argument are not difficult to discern. Terrorism certainly causes fear on the part of ordinary people, but fear of the terrorists themselves. If anything, terrorism tends to drive people more firmly into the arms of their government. The classic case of this is the terror bombing of Germany in the Second World War, whose intention was to drive a wedge between Hitler and his people. However, the effect was just the opposite. Hitler could plausibly say to his people that only monsters would rain down fire upon innocent people and that he was their only refuge from barbarism. The same analysis applies to modern terrorism. One has only to look at the areas of the world where terror has held sway to see that typically terrorism prolongs conflict, sometimes seemingly without end. Whether it be in Ireland or the Middle East, terrorism creates a climate of fear such that no one feels safe unless the opponent is totally destroyed. In this sense, terrorism declares 'total' war because no one is exempt from attack and no one is innocent. In such an ethos, compromise and negotiation become impossible. Who can negotiate with barbarians?

Finally, is the short cut argument ever advanced non-hypocritically? It is always difficult to determine motives, but noting the historic failure of the argument, one suspects that what matters to people about to embark upon a terrorist operation is not the moral calculus involving the net beneficial consequences of terrorism, but rather a prior decision to wage war the cheapest way possible. For terrorism, whether of the Second World War variety or the most recent outbreaks of the IRA, is war on the cheap. When that decision is made the moral justification of more lives saved is got up as an afterthought.

Recognition in some quarters that terrorism cannot be morally justified and that direct attacks upon innocent people are counterproductive has caused some terrorist groups to shift to a strategy of assassination. The Provisional Irish Republican Army and the Puerto Rican separatist group FALN are examples of those who argue that as they attack only representatives of the 'oppressive regime' their use of force satisfies legal constraints of discrimination and proportionality; indeed, they will argue that assassination is the most discriminate of all forms of violence.

While we should perhaps be grateful for any efforts at discrimination on the part of terrorist groups, however motivated, assassination does have serious moral problems. First, the targets selected by terrorists are typically ordinary police officers, civil servants, judges, politicians and so on. Now the modern bureaucratic state employs a large number of people who may or may not have anything to do with making policy (even less so than, say, a journalist) so that some of these killings are inevitably going to be 'symbolic', not, in other words, acts of self-defence against the victim himself but against him as representative of government policy. More generally, assassination differs from combat morally in that while the latter involves self-defence against direct attacks upon life, the former involves a political judgement about the complicity of the victim in an unjust policy. To that extent assassination is morally risky in a way that combat is not.

This is not to say that assassination is not ever morally justified. If Hitler had been killed in 1940, there would have been general applause all round.

But it is perfectly clear that the kind of revolutionary violence implied by assassination could be justified only as a last resort. Therefore, the claims of groups such as the IRA and FALN to moral respectability as revolutionaries, not as terrorists, totally fail. For such violence could be justified only in a situation of extreme repression where there were no alternatives to the gun. But what sorts of regime are, in fact, the targets of modern terrorist groups? Certainly not the Soviet Union, China, or any other totalitarian state. Rather, terrorists operate exclusively against liberal democratic states: Germany, France, Italy, the USA, India, Great Britain. The argument for assassination and revolutionary violence has no validity in a democratic state. Take the case of the IRA. The political wing of the IRA, Sinn Fein, is a legal political party in Northern Ireland which regularly runs candidates for national and local office; the ballot box is open to all, there is a free press, an independent judiciary, free speech and freedom of movement. What conceivable last resort argument for assassination could be made in this context? The same analysis would apply to FALN assassinations of FBI agents and US servicemen.

As the main thrust of contemporary terrorism is the destabilization of liberal democratic states, no moral capital is to be made, no gain in moral respectability, by a transition to policies of assassination. Democracy is the most just of all decision procedures because each person is given an equal share of political power – one man, one vote. By attacking the representatives of a democratic state, the terrorist is demanding more political power than is rightly his and his actions may be described as the essence of unjust force.

Terrorism is, in the end, a form of psychological warfare. Statistically, the number of people killed is small. The main effect of terrorism is not physical, but psychological damage of a sort which tears at the very fabric of democratic society. In effect, the terrorist announces that the whole world is a Hobbesian state of nature, that there is no civil order, that the state cannot protect its people. Thus, terrorism does strike some of our most deep-seated fears about the fragility of society, particularly modern society. To fight this threat we will need not only force but knowledge of the nature of the threat as well as carefully crafted moral refutations of the pretentious claims of the terrorists.

PART II
Protest

6. Rawls in the Nonideal World: an Evaluation of the Rawlsian Account of Civil Disobedience

David Gosling

I

The Rawlsian account of civil disobedience

Despite disagreement about the qualities and defects of Rawls's *A Theory of Justice*, there is nevertheless general agreement that it is a classic expression of liberal ideals. His treatment of civil disobedience is clearly in sympathy with a generation of liberal political theorists (see for example Bedau 1961; Brown 1961; Wasserstrom 1961; Dworkin 1968; Macfarlane 1968; Martin 1969; Hall 1971; Woozley 1976) and was considered, in the words of one reviewer in the liberal tradition, to be 'the nearest thing we have yet to an adequate account of these subtle matters' (Feinberg 1973). Rawls followed the liberal tradition by arguing that in societies which have established institutional controls to protect the individual from substantial injustice and adequate processes to bring about reform by means of democratic elections, citizens have a *prima facie* moral obligation to obey the law. Intentional disobedience to achieve political purposes, therefore, requires exceptional circumstances to justify overriding the political obligation normally required of citizens in Western democracies and must conform to restrictive conditions.

In Rawls's case the role assigned to civil disobedience is closely bound up with his anxieties about the possible outcomes of majority rule and his commitment to the priority of liberty.[1] He believes that by having civil disobedience as a last resort appeal addressed to the final authority of the sovereign people, the stability of a just constitution may be maintained against the possible abuse of majority power. Individuals have the right to resist injustice because society is to be interpreted as a scheme of 'cooperation among equals', and therefore 'those injured by serious injustice need not submit' (Rawls 1972: 383).

On the one hand, then, Rawls is concerned to allow direct action to further justice in a nonideal world. However, on the other hand, he does not want such action to be a threat to the stability of what he takes to be nearly just societies. He therefore only allows that civil disobedience is justified when there is 'substantial and clear injustice', and two provisos have been met, first, that normal appeals to the political majority have already been made in good faith and have failed and, secondly, that the actions engaged in do not lead to a breakdown in the respect for the law and the constitution (373–4). Rawls's definition of civil disobedience as a 'conscientious yet political act contrary to the law usually done with the aim of bringing about a change in law or policies of the government' has within it still more restrictions; it must be public, which he interprets as requiring that fair notice be given of the protest to the authorities, and nonviolent (364). The dissenter must offer him or herself up to the authorities in order to take the legal consequences, and cannot appeal to principles of private morality but only to the public concept of justice. Wherever this is not clear, for example, on taxation policy, civil disobedience is not appropriate (372).

'So understood', says Rawls, 'a conception of civil disobedience is part of the theory of free government' (385). Illegal forms of protest have a constitutional role providing these conditions are fulfilled. In return for the restraint showed by protesters the courts should take into account the conscientious nature of the act and on these grounds reduce or suspend legal sanction.

As this is the only question of 'nonideal theory' pursued in any detail in the book,[2] we are, I think, justified in testing the principles he enunciates in the light of our experience. I shall take the view that Rawls's continued references to 'nearly just states', and to institutions which are 'reasonably just' or which 'do not exceed the limits of tolerable injustice' (for example Rawls 1972: 363) give us the right to examine the application of his view of civil disobedience to actual democratic states. I shall assume initially that the United Kingdom is one such state with institutions that are sufficiently 'nearly just' and with a sufficient commitment to Rawls's two principles of justice to allow an examination of his view of civil disobedience in the context of British experience. Although this assumption may not be sustainable, it is worth pointing out that, since Rawls (363) makes it clear he does not intend his theory to apply to unjust states, if the requirements for a 'nearly just' state are interpreted too stringently,[3] the theory will turn out not to have application to any actual state, with the paradoxical implication that there never has been civil disobedience in Rawls's sense.[4]

It is my contention that when we do try to apply Rawls's concept of civil disobedience in the nonideal world we find a fundamental incoherence in it. In a 'nearly just state' there is nevertheless sufficient injustice to warrant resistance, but not enough injustice to warrant its being destabilized. Yet the same state machinery that has been found lacking in responding to the clear and substantial injustice is expected to show tolerance and leniency to those who reveal its inadequacies. This displays the unresolved tension between radical and conservative rhetorics in liberal theory which leaves the status and role of civil disobedience ambiguous and uncertain. Furthermore, the 'fair play' foundation upon which the argument is built cannot bear the weight. The liberal state turns out to be neither as homogenous in its sense of justice as Rawls requires, nor as tolerant of dissent as he desires, and as a result, I shall argue, justified civil disobedience cannot be as constrained as Rawls suggests it should be if it is to play a significant role in resisting injustice.

I shall proceed by challenging some key aspects of Rawls's restricted concept of civil disobedience, by questioning the requirement that justified disobedience must appeal to the public conception of justice. Finally I shall examine the application of Rawls's theory to political reality by examining the status of civil disobedience in the United Kingdom.

II

The concept of civil disobedience

The category of political disobedience may range from civil war and terrorism at one extreme to the nonviolent breach of a minor law as a token protest (such as a pavement sitdown or painting a slogan). It is necessary to distinguish between acts designed to subvert a political system and *civil* disobedience, where 'civility' implies a recognition of the general obligations of citizenship, in particular a respect for others' rights. Rawls attempts to capture this distinction by defining types of disobedience which nevertheless maintain 'fidelity to the law' but, I shall argue, limiting civil disobedience in line with these stipulations would considerably limit its political effectiveness as a form of protest.

First, *publicity*. Whilst for civil disobedience to function as a *political* act it must be addressed to the public, it is not necessary that every aspect of it should be in the public arena. In particular the requirement that protesters give fair notice to the authorities of a civilly disobedient protest is too strong, since to do so may enable police action to prevent the protest.[5] The sense in which the protest is disobedient may be in its not having the police permission required by law, and therefore 'due notice' would destroy its impact. Does Rawls assume that the authorities would not take actions to thwart the intention of the protesters once public notice had been given? Where wide powers are granted to the police to place restrictive conditions on even those protests allowed by law the incentive for dissenting groups to cooperate with the police in the way suggested inevitably diminishes.

Second, *nonviolence*. Whilst Rawls is right to maintain that non-violence is generally vastly superior to violent action both as the most effective strategy to win public support, and in terms of moral quality, an action is not necessarily transformed from civil disobedience into subversion by virtue of there being violence against person or property. The cogency of a protest is not necessarily lost by its being violent, nor does a protest that *becomes* violent in response to police action against the protesters lose its status as civil disobedience. All civil disobedience necessarily causes some disruption or inconvenience to others, and to that extent involves a degree of coercion,[6] but what distinguishes civil disobedience from terrorist subversion is that the former is concerned to bring attention to a specific wrong that is believed to exist and not to undermine the authority of the government. Actions, whether violent or not, which breach fundamental moral rights of security from physical harm to person and property do require a more stringent justification than those which do not, but either the violence used against protesters or the extent of the wrong which is the object of the protest may in specific contexts provide such a justification (see Morreall 1976; Smart 1978; Honderich 1980).

Third, *acceptance of punishment*. The acceptance of punishment may be a useful tactic to bring publicity through court hearings, but it does not follow that because a group chooses a different strategy it is necessarily withdrawing its fidelity to the law in general in matters outside the scope of the protest. When there is a lack of faith in the fairness of law enforcement, or when the law being breached is itself thought to be unjust, an unwillingness to put oneself in the hands of the police is justifiable. (For example a young black male protesting against police discrimination may be justified in being less willing to offer himself up for arrest than, say, a group of middle class professional people protesting about the line of a road or a site for the dumping of nuclear waste.) Individuals cannot be expected to cooperate with institutions perceived to be implicated in their own repression.

Fourth, the appeal must be to the *sense of justice* of the majority of the community. Rawls believes that unless protesters can appeal to the sense of justice of the 'larger society' the majority may respond with more repressive measures against the minority (Rawls 1972: 386–7), but even if this may be so we may nevertheless question whether this is a necessary condition of civil disobedience. The nature of the wrongs in government policy to which civil disobedience is designed to draw attention may include policy issues which raise matters of moral concern, but which are not obviously issues of justice as such. Disputes over environmental issues such as nuclear power, blood sports, the treatment of animals in factory farms, and nuclear deterrence are not about the justice of government policies but about the moral issues they raise.[7] Admittedly any matter of morality may be described within a rights-based discourse and as such may be brought under a discussion of justice, but only at the price of trivializing the concept of justice. Furthermore, addressing the sense of justice of the majority of the community seems to rule out the possibility of protests which attempt to mould and alter the prevailing public conception of justice as the suffragettes did, or animal rights protesters attempt to do today.[8] Moral limits on the methods of justified protest are necessary (in order to distinguish civil disobedience from terrorism), but to put a ban on all issues other than those which can appeal to the existing sense of justice reflects, as Barry (1973: 152) has suggested, a faith in the sentiments of the members of a nearly just society not justified by experience.

The requirement that protest must be against 'substantial' injustice seems not to allow for the possibility that comparatively minor violations of individual rights can accumulate into substantial losses of liberty unless they are resisted.[9] Citizens may find their right to dissent rendered ineffective if minor breaches are allowed to go unprotested on too many occasions.[10] Where a wrong is perceived and the normal channels for bringing about change are likely to be too slow or unresponsive because the institutions for reform are controlled by those sympathetic to the government, civil disobedience may be necessary before 'substantial injustice' occurs, since it is better to prevent the suffering that injustice necessarily entails than to respond to injustice when it has already become entrenched.

Also problematic is the restraint that Rawls urges when other minorities have an equal right to resort to disobedience leading to a possible breakdown of respect for the law, since it requires any one group to modify its actions in the light of the mere possibility of other groups failing to exercise the same restraint. Should animal rights campaigners take into account what antinuclear protesters, or religious minority groups, might or might not do? Admittedly it may be tactically inadvisable to use disobedience at a time when the public's, government's or police's tolerance is wearing thin. Protesters have a duty to consider the consequences of their actions and should heed Hume's warning:

> Where a disposition to rebellion appears among any people, it is one chief cause of tyranny in the rulers, and forces them into many violent measures which they never would have embraced, had everyone been inclined to submission and obedience. (Hume 1963: 475)

But we must distinguish between the moral grounds of a protest and a consideration of its likely consequences, for a civilly disobedient protest may be quite justified and yet tactically misconceived and potentially counterproductive. Rawls wishes to impose this restriction in order to prevent a 'breakdown in the respect for law and the constitution' (Rawls 1972: 373). But if there are so many cases of 'minorities justified in engaging in civil disobedience' it may be that the state has already departed from the position of 'near justice', in which case the restraints on 'civil' disobedience do not apply and what Rawls calls 'militant' action may be justified. In any case the threat of a general breakdown in obedience to the law is often invoked when the likelihood of its happening is remote.[11]

Rather than confuse stipulation with substantive moral claims, it is preferable, I believe, to work with a minimal definition of civil disobedience and not attempt to specify a set of restrictive conditions, in order not to foreclose on issues of justification and strategy.[12] We may, I suggest, define civil disobedience as a form of protest characterized by the following necessary and jointly sufficient conditions: (1) the intention to act illegally (to distinguish disobedience from legal forms of protest),[13] (2) the motivation to influence, or express a moral position on, a matter of public policy or law (to bring out the political and moral character of civil disobedience) and (3) two kinds of limitation, (i) the limited goal which the action seeks to achieve, and (ii) the limited methods used which are bounded by a recognition of the fundamental rights of other citizens within a community (to distinguish such actions from wide-scale subversion, rebellion or treason).[14] For the purposes of this discussion I propose that these three conditions give us an adequate conception of civil disobedience, which does not rule out examples normally thought to fall under this concept and which leaves open the question of when the resort to disobedience is justified.

III

Disobedience in a pluralist society

A central plank to the liberal defence of limited disobedience is the distinction between actions motivated by a conscientious concern for the defence of what Rawls calls the sense of justice of the majority and actions motivated by self or group interest. A legitimate concern here is that any justification of disobedience should not endorse attempts by individuals or groups to advantage themselves unfairly by coercion of the majority. For example workers in key industries such as the generation of electricity are not justified in using their industrial power to give themselves unfair advantages. But the Rawlsian appeal to a public conception of justice is not a coherent way to guard against unjustified disobedience. As Walzer (1983: 79) for example has argued, as soon as we move away from the hypothetical abstraction of the 'original position' into the real world of political choice it becomes implausible to suggest that there is anything approaching a common sense of justice. Over issues such as the distribution of wealth, the level of taxation, the place of religion in society, trade union rights, the appropriate balance between private and public ownership, the implementation of equality of opportunity, the value to be placed on education, the rights of women, just to name a few, there are widely differing views in the democratic marketplace.

The fact that certain views are dominant and are implemented by government at any given time does not at all entail the existence of a consensus, or even of a majority view. The ascendance of a particular political stance has more to do with the contingencies of economics, personalities, and the power of opinion formers than to any settled view of justice. The public sense of justice to which Rawls requires all civil disobedience to appeal is not the rational monolithic edifice Rawls constructs but is made up of fragmented, contradictory, intuitive, unsystematic beliefs within wide variations of class-based, religious, cultural and ethnic practices. Individuals and groups perceive their place within the society from the perspective of a particular set of values and commitments, some relatively fixed and others shifting in response to pressures and influences.[15]

In denying a place for self or group interest in civil disobedience Rawls writes as though individuals and groups survey the nearly just society from some wholly neutral position, being concerned only to improve the fairness of the whole by correcting particular malformations of administrative or legal procedures. Such altruistically motivated disobedience does occur, but the majority of acts of disobedience are differently motivated, emerging as they do from particular viewpoints within subcultures with their own standards, values and priorities. It is when these commitments are challenged or denied by legislation, or by the enforcement agencies of government, that people rebel – not in the name of the society as a whole, but in protection of what they hold dear. To assign legitimacy only to disobedience concerned with fidelity to some abstract model of justice denies the social and constitutional importance of all those cases where individuals or groups are concerned only to rectify what they perceive as a wrong that affects their own way of life.

Grunwick and Wapping; Brixton, Toxteth, Broadwater Farm; the students on Westminster Bridge; Kent householders; the peace convoy on Salisbury Plain; rooftop protests and hunger strikes in prisons, bookburning by Muslims – these among many others are examples of protests that became disobedient (though with different degrees of civility) and which represent very different interest groups within society – trade unionists, ethnic minorities, students, middle class residents, travellers, prisoners and Muslims. Each believed it had genuine grievances which affected its rights, each was defending group interests, each believed that the state had failed to provide adequate protection or adequate legal means of pursuing its claims. Of course the rights and wrongs of each of these causes is debatable, but it cannot be denied that they have a place in the political debate simply because they did not appeal to the common sense of justice. Rawls is by his rhetoric, if not by intention, denying the value of disobedience which is expressive of a person's sense that the dominant forces of society, even within a nearly just and nearly democratic society, are alien to their ethical concerns.[16] Such protests enable otherwise marginal groups to contribute to the public debate and afford them the possibility of an impact on policy-making which the different levels of access to influence within society normally does not allow. Many minority groups with defensible rights cannot rely on the media, political parties or legal authorities to represent their views adequately or forcibly[17] and, with narrowed definitions of legal protests, it becomes more likely that attempts to make an impact on public debate will be regarded as disobedient.

These examples illustrate that the distinction between a sense of justice and self-interest is not always transparent. We may nevertheless distinguish these actions from those of the criminal because they are intended to be part of a public dialogue about issues of rights and policy, and we can distinguish them from those of terrorists because the methods used are not designed to force change by coercion or terror and because such groups do not intend the overthrow of the government of the day or the rejection of the legal system as a whole. There is a fundamental difference between protest, which is the public expression of a conscientiously held belief, the passionate defence of a principle, the attempt to impress on the government and public opinion the significance of an issue to be fought for or a right to be defended, and coercion, whether violent or nonviolent, which attempts to force a change of law or policy. If, as Dworkin (1985: 110) says, 'civil disobedients remain democrats at heart' the use of coercive tactics (civil blackmail) can be justified only in circumstances when there are no alternative means of achieving or defending a fundamental democratic right. It is not justified to force a change of view in the majority. Animal rights activists are not justified in attempting to threaten the majority in order to blackmail them into becoming vegetarians, nor are Muslims justified in threatening the safety of non-Muslims in order to force the adoption of some Islamic principle, but both may find ways of expressing their beliefs in noncoercive ways to bring to the attention of the majority the importance of beliefs that would otherwise have been given little or no weight.

More problematic are actions on behalf of interest groups, such as residents, farmers, trade unionists and so on, when the intention is to alter public policy in a manner which is more favourable to the interest group concerned. Here the distinction between self-interest and a concern for justice is highly contentious, but such groups may be able to justify their actions if it can be demonstrated that a substantial democratic principle is at stake, rather than simply a matter of financial losses, or alteration of policy.

IV

The status of civil disobedience in 'nearly just' states

Let us now turn to the question of how far the legitimacy of civil disobedience has been accepted within the United Kingdom. Rawls (1972:

383–7) argues that justified disobedience by his criteria 'is one of the stabilising devices of a constitutional system', that it 'helps to maintain and strengthen just institutions', and is therefore 'part of the the theory of free government'. This has implications for the response of government to acts of justifiable conscientious disobedience, which Rawls argues should be recognized by the courts as legitimate acts by 'the principles underlying the constitution' and that therefore courts should 'on these grounds reduce and in some cases suspend the legal sanction'.

Rawls's attempt to legitimate, within strict limits, certain restricted forms of civil disobedience, has failed to convince the governments of democratic states such as the United Kingdom. On the contrary, over the last twenty years, we have seen a threefold policy – first, an increase in legislation to criminalize more forms of protest (outside wartime), second, an increasing willingness to prosecute dissenters, and third, a trend towards stricter police tactics designed to break up mass protests.[18]

In the 1980s we have seen Section 2 of the Official Secrets Act used against individuals who acted conscientiously to protect the right of Parliament to be given truthful answers by government ministers, and new legislation which specifically excludes a public interest defence. The Public Order Act 1986 requires organizers of all demonstrations to inform the police, who can impose conditions on the form of the protest to prevent serious disorder, damage to property, disruption to the life of the community, or the intimidation of others. Such catch-all wording allows senior police officers to limit protest in almost every case since some form of disruption to the community is virtually a necessary feature of any effective protest. It is also an offence to use words or behaviour which are threatening, abusive, insulting, or disorderly, and are likely to harass, alarm or distress another, even if no one was actually distressed. The traditional presumption of innocence has been dropped in this Act since it is the defendant who must prove that his behaviour is not likely to be distressing to others (see Galligan 1988).

Such legislation is indicative of government intolerance towards public protest. Clearly the state apparatus is unwilling to make fine distinctions between the motivation of dissenters, and is inclined to categorize all protest as subversive of democratic procedures. As Tucker (1980: 227) has pointed out, politicians are in a powerful ideological position to use the symbols of legitimacy and authority as important instruments for social control because they can appeal to a positive conception of correctly promulgated law. This is precisely how the clichéd invocation of the need to 'maintain law and order' is manipulated to reinforce government definitions of legitimacy. Against those who have argued that legal sanctions should be suspended when an action is conscientiously motivated,[19] governments have reiterated the principle that there cannot be degrees of illegality, which may be readily conceded, but which essentially misses the point; the illegality of civil disobedience is not after all in question, but rather what the appropriate response of authority to such acts should be.

The limitations that Rawls places on legitimate disobedience assume a corresponding willingness on the part of the state to be responsive to the demands of those protesting against perceived injustices. He nevertheless recognizes that actual governments are liable to fail in this respect, which is why civil disobedience is required precisely because legal forms of redress fail. This failure of legal channels to produce justice even within 'nearly just states' suggests the more general difficulty of the insensitivity of established institutions to dissenting groups. In a society which shares the conviction that democratic principles and rights offer the 'best bet' for citizens to protect themselves from the abuse of government authoritarianism, there is a strong interest for all in not destabilizing those institutions that offer even imperfect democratic safeguards. But when governments use the imperfections of liberal democratic procedures and institutions, supported by their near monopoly of force, to defend and further group interests, the justification for the self-imposed restraints on protest that Rawls requires becomes eroded.

This brings us to the general question of policing protests. The police are not totally insensitive to the distinction between civil and criminal disobedience, since they do sometimes prefer not to seek confrontation when they fear adverse publicity, but the overwhelming impression created by police action in recent times is a determination to restrict the impact of even the most vigorous demonstration. The police argue that it is no part of their job to make judgements about which instances of lawbreaking are justified on conscientious grounds, but alienation is intensified when police action is perceived as being selective and prejudiced. Furthermore the police must take some responsibility for the escalation of disputes when their response to an initial protest is a contributory cause to a shift towards violence. Any diminution of the confidence of the public in the police's determination to deal fairly with dissenting groups reduces the motivation of dissenters to cooperate with the process of law enforcement. When the semblance of a fair and equal system is continually challenged by apparent injustices, out-groups like ethnic minorities and travellers will perceive themselves as beyond the boundaries of the community which have an interest in obedience to the law. In this respect the police take a large responsibility for the stability of the system of public order.

Perhaps we should abandon the attempt to understand recent events within a Rawlsian framework and instead accept that there is a deep gulf between the political reality of liberal states and the Rawlsian ideal. Increasingly citizens are encouraged to think that acting in an aggressively self-interested way is both necessary for economic change and desirable socially and politically. But the apparent rejection of 'social justice' as an explicit goal of government may be taken to undermine the motivation for political obedience. As Gauthier (1977: 160) has said, 'Awareness of oneself as an appropriator undercuts one's willingness to accept the constraints of the political order'.

A society which shows little interest in rectifying inequalities and injustices loses the loyalty of those citizens who perceive themselves to be victims rather than beneficiaries of a scheme of social cooperation and increases the incidence of scepticism about the value of acting in constitutional ways. Such scepticism can issue in very diverse responses ranging from surrender to resistance, including rioting and so-called hooliganism. By increasing the policing function of the state and by a rigid refusal to enter into compromises with alternative visions of society, governments appear to aim at instilling a sense of helplessness among opposition groups that will discourage them from embarking on policies of dissent and protest. By narrowing the definition of legitimate protest the scope for effective legal participation in political processes is considerably reduced for those groups who are not substantially represented in political parties – gays, feminists, Muslims, animal rights supporters and so on. The result is, despite liberal claims about democracy, an endorsement of political apathy and a celebration of 'the silent majority' presumed to support authority, but whose main virtue is its quiescence. Those who attempt to make effective contributions to the debate by offering alternative views are simultaneously 'activists' and 'subversives', a group that in recent years has made some surprising recruits. Against this fear of 'activism' in politics 'politicization' is seen as undesirable and unnecessary, a view which underlies the suspicion of political education in secondary schools.

Whenever arguments are brought in support of disobedience and against the duty to obey there is an understandable unease that the 'rule of law' may be undermined and that citizens may be encouraged to disobey the law whenever they choose, but it does not follow that because there is no obligation to obey the law there is a right to disobey. To have a right is to have a protected sphere of action within which I may do as I wish whether it be right or wrong. No such right to disobey the law exists, for there is no right to disobey the law without justification. If I disobey with justification then the rightness of my action derives from the integral moral quality of the action (see Raz 1979: 266). If it is noble and right to do what is necessary to protect freedom of speech, to clean up the environment or rid the world of nuclear weapons, then it is tautologous to say that I have a right to do these things, whatever the legal status of those actions. If it is ugly and wrong to threaten people because I disagree with them, to incite racial hatred or to have discriminatory employment practices, then I have no right to do these things, even if the law does not forbid them. The denial of political obligation does not remove moral constraints on action – on the contrary, by recognizing the autonomy of the citizen, it puts the justification of each individual's acceptance of, or resistance to, government authority firmly within the moral sphere (see Smith 1973: 969; Simmons 1979: 193).

V

Conclusion

I have argued that, if we are to regard the United Kingdom as a nearly just state, Rawls's accounts of the conditions under which we may disobey are inadequate to the task of advancing justice, given current political and economic realities. If on the other hand the UK is not 'nearly just' then we must operate with a less restrictive notion of civil disobedience and construct different grounds for its use. The Rawlsian ideal is noble and admirable but until such time as the governments of liberal states acknowledge their role in the scheme, citizens cannot be expected to be bound by a nonvoluntary contract in which the stability it defends perpetuates injustice.[20]

Notes

1. See the discussion on 'Limitations on participation' (Rawls 1972: §37) where, for example, Rawls is prepared to countenance plural voting if that were to protect the priority of liberty. See also the discussion in Rawls 1969: 243–6.
2. See Rawls 1972: 351. The principles of justice belong to ideal theory because they assume that whatever principles are acknowledged as just in the original position will be strictly complied with. Nonideal theory is needed when there is only partial compliance, for example within a nearly just state. See Feinberg 1973.
3. Rawls merely requires that laws voted be 'within the range of those that could reasonably be favoured by rational legislators conscientiously trying to follow the principles of justice' (1972: 362). This could include a Conservative government following free market/monetarist policies, since they would ('conscientiously') argue that such policies do ultimately bring the maximum benefit to the worst off – although this may not be the prime object of their policies.
4. Barry (1973) refers to this as Rawls's 'heaven and hell conception of political possibilities'. On Rawls's difficulties in moving from his abstract account of 'ideal' theory to the real world see Haksar 1976b: 163 and Pateman 1985: 127.
5. Smart (1978: 264) makes a similar point.
6. As Macfarlane (1968: 45–6) has pointed out, nonviolent coercion can be more damaging than violence. Dworkin (1985) attempts to distinguish between persuasive and nonpersuasive methods, but the distinction cannot always be clearly drawn. See Norman 1986.
7. Dworkin (1985) attempts to distinguish between civil disobedience which involves 'convictions of principle' and that which is 'policy-based', but objections to policy (such as the use of nuclear deterrence, to take his example) will necessarily raise matters of conviction.
8. This is essentially Singer's objection. See Singer 1973: 88.
9. See Sumner's comment (1977: 28): 'Rawls' first condition leaves little room for adopting limited means to limited ends.'
10. Thornton (1989) and Dworkin (1988) argue that this has happened in the UK in the last ten years.
11. See Smith 1973: 966, Sumner 1977: 28, Wasserstrom 1980: 93–4, Zwiebach 1975: 204. All criticize the unjustified use of the generalization argument.
12. Bayles (1970), Hall (1971), and Sumner (1977) also support the idea of a minimal definition.
13. In some cases it may be unclear whether an act is illegal, and the protest may be part of a campaign to clear a point of illegality. See for example Dworkin's discussion (1977: 206 ff) of anti-Vietnam protests, where the legality of enforcing the draft was at issue. Smart (1978: 260) suggests that 'the act is regarded as illegal by at least one court and at the time of acting no higher court had decided otherwise'.
14. On this definition Gandhi's campaign of disobedience was limited in its methods but not in its aims since it sought the overthrow of the government; perhaps it should be regarded as 'civil subversion'. Smart (1978: 267) suggests that it is only when a protest combines both revolutionary aims and coercion by violence that it fails to be civil disobedience.
15. On the inability of the state to be the appropriate location for moral consensus see MacIntyre 1981: 182.
16. Nor is it sufficient to put these cases into the separate category of 'conscientious refusal', for while some of these cases may involve the 'noncompliance with a more or less direct legal injunction or administrative order' most were concerned with the more positive task of establishing a right or some point of principle. See Rawls 1972: 368.

17. This was one of Russell's fundamental justifications of disobedience. On the question of British unilateralism, he argued, 'there is an entirely sober case to be made out for this policy, but the misrepresentations of opponents, who command the main organs of publicity, have made it very difficult to cause this to be known.... It has therefore seemed to some of us necessary to supplement the Campaign for Nuclear Disarmament by such actions as the press is sure to report' (Russell 1961: 246).
18. Evidence for these claims may be found in, for example, Thornton 1989, Gostin 1988 and Dworkin 1988.
19. Apart from Rawls 1972: 387, see also Dworkin 1968 and Hall 1971.
20. I should like to thank the editors for their comments on previous drafts.

7. Nuclear Energy, Value Conflicts, and the Legitimacy of Political Decisions: the Rise and Fall of an Alleged Justification for Violent Civil Disobedience

Heta Häyry and Matti Häyry

I

In March 1987 a report concerning decision-making in energy policies was published in Finland by two researchers from the Turku School of Economics, Pentti Malaska and Pirkko Kasanen (Malaska and Kasanen 1987). The research was financed by the Finnish Ministry of Commerce and Industry, and was seen by many as an official statement from the public authorities. The overt bias against the use of nuclear energy displayed in the report was strongly attacked by all those who hold the view that Finland – now the possessor of four nuclear power plants – will in the near future need a fifth unit to produce what they refer to as 'cheap and clean energy'.

The report was thoroughly peer-reviewed prior to its publication, and there was intensive public debate over its contents in the spring of 1987. We have elsewhere (Häyry and Häyry 1989) reported in more detail precisely what was said in the discussion and by whom, but finer details are not necessary for our purposes in this paper.

II

The point of the original report was roughly the following. The models that are currently used in economic and political decision-making, standard democratic procedures, only work properly as long as a value consensus prevails. The questions surrounding decision-making on national energy policies involve, however, deep and irreconcilable value conflicts. This is shown in the report by comparing, in what the authors call 'cognitive maps', the statements of those for and those against the use of nuclear energy in Finland. Clearly different life values are represented when the opposing parties evaluate the consequences of pro- and antinuclear decisions.

The argument of the report can be presented in syllogistic form as follows:

(P1) Current models of democratic decision-making only work properly if a value consensus prevails with regard to the consequences of alternative decisions.

(P2) Deep value conflicts prevail, however, with regard to the consequences of alternative (nuclear) energy policy decisions.

(CL) Therefore, current models of democratic decision-making do not work properly in (nuclear) energy policy issues.

The authors draw two important corollaries from the conclusion. One of them is, of course, that under the present circumstances new models of decision-making are badly needed. As to the precise nature of these new procedures, only hints are given in the report, but the authors have since continued their work in that direction (Malaska, Kantola and Kasanen1989; see also Häyry, Häyry and Rossilahti forthcoming). However, the other main corollary drawn from the conclusion is of more interest to us here: the authors imply that the inadequacy of energy policy decisions in the present value conflict situation justifies active resistance against the implementation of decisions to employ (more) nuclear energy. And since 'active resistance' in the context of the report probably means acts of civil disobedience or sabotage, the theory of decision-making presented by the authors must be seen, at least partly, as an attempt to legitimate such acts.[1]

III

Now let us sketch an example or two of the kinds of act opponents of nuclear energy production might have in mind when they are dissatisfied with current policies.

One characteristic incident might be that a group of concerned citizens chain themselves to the gates of a nuclear power station when a new supply of uranium is known to be coming to the plant. This kind of action, if and when it occurs, usually fulfils the standard criteria of civil disobedience: it is intentional, public, symbolic and presumably illegal (Smart 1978). It may or may not be violent, depending on the actual behaviour of the demonstrators, and on the consequences of their action. Innocent by-standers can be indirectly harmed by the act if, for instance, domestic or industrial areas are left without electricity for significant periods of time because of the demonstration. In such a case civil disobedience would, although indirectly, be violent in the sense that it might damage property, and perhaps cause harm to people.

However, the use of the term 'active resistance' in the report seems to imply that the authors also see in their theory a justification for more straightforward attacks. Another way in which opponents of nuclear power might wish to make their point is by attempting to slow down power production in a given plant. This could be done either by destroying vital machinery and equipment or by threatening, harming, or curtailing the liberty of those working in the power plant. In both cases violence either against property or against persons would be inevitable. These acts of sabotage and assault, as well as acts of expressive civil disobedience, can and should be included in the sphere of active resistance.

But assuming that this is a fair interpretation of what is said in the report, problems begin to accumulate at this point. It is difficult to see how standard justifications of civil disobedience and subversion could be employed in the situations described. Public decisions concerning nuclear energy policies have as a rule been reached through constitutional proce-dures; they do not overtly violate citizens' basic legal rights; they are not usually in violation of relevant international treaties or regulations; and the existence of nuclear power plants does not normally create immediate risks which would render direct action legitimate as the only way to prevent great disasters.

As the authors point out, however, this is not necessarily how opponents of nuclear energy see the matter. They may argue that the legitimacy of decisions is an illusion, created by people whose values are radically different from those of their own. And this disagreement concerning values, they may further argue, is what justifies active resistance. If the argument presented in the report holds, standard justifications of civil disobedience and subversion are not needed in situations where basic values are in conflict.

The question, then, is whether the argument is sound and whether it can be used to support civil resistance. Our claim in this paper is that although both premises of the argument can be defended against some attacks at least, they can be defended only at the cost of fatally weakening their original strength with regard to the second main corollary of the argument.

IV

One obvious way to undermine the argument of the report is to question its first premise (Pl). Since there are nearly always conflicting interests involved in political decision-making, it is necessary for the proponent of the view to distinguish between *interests* and *values,* and to maintain that whereas conflicting interests can legitimately be reconciled by standard democratic procedures, conflicting values cannot. Without such a distinction the argument would amount to saying that current methods of decision-making virtually never work properly. And that claim, even if it were true in some sense, would hardly make a good case in defence of potentially violent acts of civil disobedience and subversion. It should be borne in mind that the authors of the report are not advocating a full-scale revolution or mutiny: their complaint is restricted to policy decisions concerning nuclear power production and other similar issues that are relevant.

The difficulty is acknowledged in the report, and the theory formulated accordingly. Values, as opposed to interests, are defined as 'goods which cannot be exchanged with other goods, or cannot be properly compensated for if they are eliminated'. Thus, if there are two travellers who both have an equal interest in having the only room in the hotel with a view, the conflict can probably be solved by compensating the losing party by, for instance, a price reduction. But if somebody were to prove that the wealth of nations is likely to increase considerably if foreign travel is completely forbidden, many of us would no doubt feel that the loss of liberty would not and indeed could not be compensated for by adding to our material welfare. There seem indeed to be goods which simply cannot be traded with other goods.

V

Let us, for the time being, assume that the first premise of the argument is true with these qualifications – that current procedures of democratic decision-making can function properly only as long as no value conflicts are involved. The next question is whether or not the second premise (P2) is true. Are there genuine value conflicts – as opposed to mere conflicts of interest – in issues related to nuclear power production?

In the report an affirmative answer is given on the ground that the opposing parties of the Finnish nuclear energy debate systematically refer to different and mutually incompatible ideals in justifying their own views. 'Proponents' usually refer to benefits such as steady economic growth, high employment rates and general welfare, which are supposed to be achieved by using nuclear power. 'Opponents', on the other hand, stress the risks and threats which in their view are causally connected with the employment of atomic energy. These include the possible harm inflicted on present or future generations by catastrophes like Harrisburg and Chernobyl, and the potential loss of civil liberties due to the increased security requirements in society at large, which are needed in order to prevent sabotage to vulnerable atomic energy plants.

Obviously, as at least one Finnish commentator has noted (Kauko Aronen, unpublished comments on Malaska and Kasanen 1987), there is the possibility of a vicious circle here: acceptance of atomic power leads to fear of sabotage, fear of sabotage leads to loss of liberty, loss of liberty contributes to the creation of a value conflict, and the value conflict justifies active resistance. In this scheme, the opponents of nuclear power can supposedly justify violence by presenting the rest of society with threats of violence in the initial decision-making situation. And it ought to be clear that this sort of self-fulfilling deduction, or an 'argument from blackmail', would be ethically unacceptable.

It is not, however, necessary to interpret the point of the report in this manner. The authors may equally well wish to make the prediction that, once in action, nuclear power plants will probably attract the attention of outside saboteurs: hostile foreign governments, criminal organizations, terrorist groups and other parties, whose goal would not be the closure of nuclear power plants. According to this interpretation, no attempt is made in the report to legitimate 'extrinsic' violence, whereas 'intrinsic' civil resistance is justified by the argument from value conflicts. Since, however, justification by no means implies live action, no prediction as to active resistance by opponents of nuclear power is necessarily made. And if this account, rather than the more cynical view, is correct, then the argument survives the attack.

VI

It seems plausible enough to claim that general welfare and personal autonomy may well be values which for certain groups of people cannot rationally be exchanged for other goods and cannot properly be compensated for. Thus genuine value conflicts do occur in issues related to energy policy. But a new question now arises. Even if we take it for granted that most political compromises only concern conflicting interests, there may be political issues of a similar nature to energy problems which have been dealt with, perhaps quite legitimately, by using standard procedures of decision-making. And it may be that in some of these issues blank acceptance of active resistance would not appear to be such a good idea after all. If this is the case, then comparisons between different debates may prove interesting.

VII

An example will elucidate the point. Whenever abortion is publicly discussed in the Western world, two rival views immediately emerge. On the one hand, there is a group of people who maintain that the sanctity of unborn human life is of such great value that it cannot be forfeited on almost any grounds. On the other hand, there are those who say that feminine autonomy clearly overrides all other values at stake. Presumably the correct interpretation here is that a genuine value conflict prevails, and that, accordingly, nonstandard procedures should be used in decision-making.

Turning, however, more specifically to the Finnish situation, on which the report is based, it is quickly revealed that no 'nonstandard' measures have been employed in deciding abortion policies in Finland. The Abortion Act of 1970 – in which the Parliament provided the nation with a moderately liberal set of regulations – was preceded by the report of an expert committee and by a spirited public debate, but these hardly count as nonstandard measures in democratic decision-making. It seems, then, that according to the argument from value conflicts the opponents of legal abortions are justified in actively resisting and obstructing their provision.

VIII

Since comparisons like this are not directly dealt with in the report, it is not absolutely certain how the authors would respond to the challenge. The alternatives logically open to them are, first, to show a relevant difference between the cases of nuclear energy and abortion, and, secondly, to argue that conflicting values in both cases actually do justify active resistance. It may be that the authors would like to take a liberal stand on the abortion issue, and therefore choose the discriminatory alternative. But it may equally well be that they are prepared to hold on to their view concerning nuclear energy even if it meant pressures towards antiliberal conclusions on other issues.

IX

Three claims can be made in favour of the discriminatory alternative. These are:

1. that there are no conflicting values in the abortion issue.
2. that the value conflicts in the two issues are formally different from each other.
3. that the value conflicts in the two issues are substantially different from each other.

If any one of these claims is both true and relevant, then the argument from value conflicts is saved.

Unfortunately for the view, however, this is not the case. As regards statements (1) and (2), we have already shown that in the formal sense – that is, according to the definition given in the report – there are conflicting values in the abortion issue just as there are conflicting values in the nuclear energy issue. If welfare and liberty are 'goods which cannot be exchanged with other goods, or cannot be properly compensated for if they are eliminated', then the same is true of the sanctity of unborn human life and the value of feminine reproductive freedom.

Claim (3), on the other hand, is obviously true, since one can hardly assume that precisely the same values are at stake in each and every contentious issue in political life. But the relevance of its truth is not at all clear. If the architects of the view reserve to themselves the right to decide which values count in applying the argument, there is really no need to discuss the merits of the argument any more. The conclusion could be reached much more economically simply by stating that some nuclear energy-related prospects are so horrible that atomic power production cannot be accepted under any circumstances. But this, of course, would beg precisely the question we are attempting to answer here, namely: Why not say the same about, for instance, liberal abortion policies?

X

.The one argument the authors implicitly present in favour of the discriminatory view is an appeal to differences in the kinds of risk attached to different activities. According to this appeal, the nuclear energy issue is unique in that an affirmative decision will permanently alter the 'risk structure' in the world: for instance, if we decide to continue using nuclear power, future generations will have to live with the problems of nuclear waste whether they prefer short-term economic welfare to other values or not. Other political decisions, important as they may be, do not have such effects, and so the opponents of nuclear power can hold on to the claim that their cause is of a different magnitude to controversies such as the abortion issue.

But although one may tend to sympathize with the authors' concern for the wellbeing of future generations, it is quite impossible to use this concern to support the argument from value conflicts. The argument, as formulated in the report, is supposed to be neutral with regard to the specific values referred to, whereas talk about avoiding certain given kinds of risk already presupposes a stand taken against those kinds of risk. After all, using the authors' logic, a negative nuclear energy decision would imply that future generations must live with the problems of economic underdevelopment whether they prefer other values to short-term welfare or not. The only difference between the cases is that only one of them happens to match the authors' own values.

XI

It seems clear enough that it is not legitimate to choose a set of particular personal values to serve as the basis for one's ethical arguments. Yet, it could be claimed to be considerably more legitimate to name a few general values, and use them as cornerstones for one's views. And what is more,

the latter approach could well be employed in defending the nondiscrimi-
natory view of value conflicts – in attacking both nuclear energy and free
abortions at the same time.

But how could one argue for the view that conflicting values justify
active resistance both in the case of nuclear energy and in the case of
abortion? An example will once again be required.

A strictly conservative 'green' view, not altogether unknown in Finland (Linkola 1986), would state that *life* is the most valuable thing in this
world, and overrides all minor values such as freedom of choice, personal
happiness and the flourishing of the human species. Given this axiology,
the best solution to the problems of modern Western societies would be to
give all power to those who would use it to conserve life whenever they can,
and this also applies to the nuclear energy and abortion issues. Since other
values would within this view be subordinated to the value of physical life,
or survival, it would not make sense to argue against it that the result would
be a totalitarian government ruled by a handful of fanatics. From the
outside, of course, the solution could be seen in a different light.

XII

Our main objection to the conservative 'green' view in this context is not,
however, that it would in real life lead to unthinkable political oppression
– although it probably would – but that it would theoretically, from the
viewpoint of the argument from value conflicts, imply the acceptance of
intolerable value despotism. It could, of course, be the case that survival is
the most important value overall, and that all human action should in the
end be guided by its recognition. But if this is the case, then there is no room
left for the view that value conflicts justify active resistance. Even if a very
large group of people held that, say, personal autonomy and short-term
welfare cannot be exchanged for survival, their views could not be taken
into account if survival were to be regarded as the only good with any real
importance.

More generally, what we have just said about placing ethical weight
only on simple survival also holds true with regard to any other constella-
tion of values that a particular group of people comes to consider as
possessing ultimate importance. An exclusive view of basic values automatically rules out the possibility of taking deep conflicts of opinion into
account in the way presumed in the report. The scope of nontradable goods

simply cannot be limited to a few basic values without losing the openness and point of the original argument.

XIII

What we have shown in this paper is that the argument put forward by Pentti Malaska and Pirkko Kasanen in their report does not support the corollary that democratic pro-nuclear decisions would, in the present circumstances, justify violent or potentially violent resistance against the employment of atomic power. We have not shown – or attempted to show – that active resistance to nuclear power production would not, in the end, actually be justifiable. Other lines of argument may, for all we know, be successfully pursued to reveal that there are flaws in the workings of democracy serious enough to provoke legitimate civil disobedience and subversion. But whatever the case may be, one thing is clear: even if an acceptable justification for active resistance could be found, 'value conflicts', as defined in the report, would form no part of its defence.[2]

Notes

1. As a matter of fact, what is explicitly said in the report is that if opponents of nuclear energy do not have their own way in political bargaining, they may drift into active resistance when the decisions are implemented. But this cannot be a genuine prediction, since it will be up to the opponents themselves whether they involve themselves in active resistance or not. Therefore, the factual approach is not open to the authors of the report. (See section V.)
2. Our thanks are due to Martin Warner for his critical comments, and to Mark Shackleton, Lecturer in English, University of Helsinki, for revising the language of the paper.

8. The Sounds of Silence

Susan Mendus

I

Three forms of silence

The aim of this paper is to consider the significance of three forms of silence: the silence which may indicate that an opinion or belief has not received a fair hearing; the silence which is claimed by an individual as an extension of the right to free speech; and the silence which is claimed as part of the right (or privilege) against self-incrimination.

The first form of silence is discussed by Bertrand Russell in his writings on civil disobedience. Speaking of British nuclear policies, Russell says:

> Where the truth is difficult to ascertain there is a natural inclination to trust the official authorities. This is especially the case when what they assert enables people to dismiss uneasiness as needlessly alarmist. The major organs of publicity feel themselves part of the Establishment and are very reluctant to take a course which the Establishment will frown on. Long and frustrating experience has proved, to those among us who have endeavoured to make unpleasant facts known, that orthodox methods alone are insufficient. By means of civil disobedience, a certain kind of publicity becomes possible.... Speaking for myself, I regard this as the most important reason for adopting civil disobedience. (As quoted in Singer 1973: 73–4.)

Russell, then, claims that in some circumstances the principle of free speech is not enough to overcome inequalities of power and that, when that is so, civil disobedience may be justified as a means of obtaining a fair hearing for an opinion which would not otherwise be heard. Here, the sounds of silence are sounds which may provide a case for adopting 'unorthodox methods' against the organs of publicity and against the Establishment.

The second form of silence, far from being an indication that free speech is not enough, is itself a form of speech. This is the silence claimed in the United States under the First Amendment, and an example of it is the

1943 *Barnette* case, in which a group of Jehovah's Witnesses challenged the constitutionality of a state requirement that children in public schools salute and pledge loyalty to the United States flag. The Supreme Court upheld their case on the grounds that the students had a right not to be compelled to affirm beliefs they did not hold. It declared:

> If there is any fixed star in our constitutional constellation, it is that no official, high or petty, can prescribe what shall be orthodox in politics, nationalism, religion, or other matters of opinion, or force citizens to confess by word or act their faith therein. (As quoted in Barendt 1985: 63.)

As Barendt remarks, 'it seems fairly clear that the Supreme Court considered that a right not to speak, in particular a right not to be forced to say what a person does not accept, is an integral aspect of freedom of speech'. This, then, is a case in which silence is construed as itself a form of speech: the right to free speech covers the right not to say (or be forced to say) what one does not believe.

The third form of silence is that which may be claimed by a defendant in a criminal trial. In Britain, such silence is protected by the common law privilege against self-incrimination, and in the United States it is protected by the constitutional right of silence under the Fifth Amendment. Such a right was recently claimed by Oliver North during the 'Irangate' hearings. It was also invoked during the McCarthy 'witch hunt' trials of the 1940s and 1950s, in response to the notorious question: 'Are you now or have you ever been a member of the Communist Party?'

Here, then, are three forms of silence: the silence which may indicate that free speech is not enough, the silence which is itself a form of speech, and the silence which a defendant may claim as a legal right or privilege. (Of course there are other forms of silence, and other cases in which silence may be claimed as a right – by the Press, by spouses as non-compellable witnesses, and so on. But I shall concentrate on these three.)

At first glance, it is hard to see anything which links these forms of silence, and indeed much has been made of the differences which divide rather than the similarities which unite them. Thus, for example, Barendt draws a sharp distinction between First and Fifth Amendment silences, noting that the former protects opinions, whereas the latter is concerned with factual information. He says:

> A right not to speak can properly only be claimed for ideas and opinions, as in the *Barnette* case itself. A right not to divulge information would often conflict with the public's more weighty interest in the disclosure of information, and

could therefore only relatively rarely be successfully asserted under a free speech provision

and he adds that:

> the right to transmit *ideas* and *views* is primarily that of the speaker; the justification for its protection is to some extent that the right is necessary to ensure the development of his individual personality; ... in contrast it is the recipient, and also the general public, who are the principal beneficiaries of the freedom to communicate *information*. (Barendt 1985: 64–5)

The distinction between opinion and information is thus closely connected with a distinction between individual self-development and the public's interest in knowing the facts. Yet the public's interest in knowing the facts is precisely the interest invoked by Russell in his defence of civil disobedience:

> the forces that control opinion are heavily weighted upon the side of the rich and powerful.... The ignorance of important public men on the subject of nuclear warfare is utterly astounding to those who have made an impartial study of the subject. And from public men this ignorance trickles down to become the voice of the people. It is against this massive artificial ignorance that our protests are directed. (As quoted in Singer 1973: 76.)

In the case of facts, information, and knowledge, the public interest takes precedence; in the case of opinion, belief, or judgement, it is the individual who has priority. Appeal to the public interest in the disclosure of information is thus prominent in recent government defences of proposed legislation which will qualify the common law privilege against self-incrimination in England and Wales. As one writer has put it, the privilege against self-incrimination is a 'guilty man's privilege' and it is hard to see why the interests of guilty men should take precedence over the more weighty public interest in bringing criminals to justice (Gerstein 1984: 248).

Of course, and as the quotation from Russell indicates, the distinction between fact and opinion may be a slender one; the opinions which we hold on issues such as nuclear defence policy are likely to be highly dependent on our understanding of the facts of the matter, and crucially informed by facts which are (or are not) made available to us. Nevertheless, the guiding principle appears to be that the pursuit of truths in which the public has a weighty interest takes priority over individual autonomy.

The sounds of silence are, therefore, of differing moral status. Silence in the case of opinions is justified in the name of individual self-development and autonomy. Silence about facts is harder to justify because of the countervailing public interest in the disclosure of information; indeed, so great is this interest that it may form the single most important defence of civil disobedience. In general, then, where truth is at stake, individual interest must give way to public interest, and silence must give way to speech; where only opinions are involved, individual self-development is sovereign.

II

Fact, opinion, and toleration

The distinction between silence about facts and silence about opinions is paralleled by a general distinction in liberalism between toleration on grounds of truth and toleration on grounds of individual self-development. In each case, toleration is justified as a *means* to something which is seen as both logically independent and of more fundamental value. Thus the argument from truth is employed by Mill in *On Liberty,* when he claims that 'all silencing of discussion is an assumption of infallibility. Its condemnation may be allowed to rest on this common argument, not the worse for being common'. (Mill 1978: 77) Twentieth-century liberals, by contrast, are far less sanguine than Mill about the possibility of attaining truth, and their argument for toleration tends to turn on individual self-development and autonomy. Thus the argument from autonomy is deemed by Joseph Raz (1986) to be the single most important liberal defence of toleration, and Ronald Dworkin (1985), whilst renouncing the use of the word 'autonomy', nevertheless justifies toleration by reference to a concept of respect for persons which has a not dissimilar Kantian ancestry.

We might expect that these general defences of toleration would extend to cover silence as well as speech. We might, in other words, expect silence to be justified to the extent that it protects and enhances individual self-development, or to the extent that it does not conflict with the pursuit of truth. And these expectations are not disappointed: as we have seen, civil disobedience is said to be justified when it serves to bring attention to important truths which will not otherwise be heard; the First Amendment is justified to the extent that it seeks to protect individual autonomy. The Fifth Amendment, however, looks less justifiable because it is sometimes invoked in an attempt to conceal important facts from the public – again, it is a guilty man's privilege, and it is hard to see why guilty men should be privileged by protection under the Fifth Amendment. In all these cases the pursuit of truth or individual self-development both ground and set limits to toleration, and it is usually by reference to these more fundamental values that the value of toleration is itself assessed.

However, the cases of silence mentioned above give rise to questions about whether these justifications of toleration are, in fact, adequate. In particular, they direct attention to a defence of toleration which moves in a quite different direction. This defence is the one provided by John Locke in his seventeenth-century *Letter Concerning Toleration*. What is interesting about Locke's account is that, although he never doubts that there are religious truths, that they are supremely important, and that it is open to people to discover them, his defence of religious toleration and its limits does not depend upon considerations of truth at all, but is concerned rather with the rationality of persecution and with the legitimate aspirations of magistrates or civil authorities.

Crudely put, Locke's argument is as follows: the state is defined in terms of the means at its disposal. These are 'to give orders by decree and compel with the sword'; 'rods and axes', 'force and blood', 'fire and the sword' are the means characteristically available to the magistrate. Yet, according to Locke, these means are not simply inefficient, but incapable of inducing genuine religious belief. They operate on the will, but belief is not subject to the will, and so those who would attempt to induce religious belief by applying the coercive means at the disposal of the state are engaged in a fundamental irrationality. They are attempting to employ a set of means inappropriate to the end which they desire to obtain.

In a recent article on Locke's *Letter* Jeremy Waldron refers to a number of ways in which Locke's account has been deemed unsatisfactory. He notes that it concentrates on the obligations of would-be persecutors, whereas modern liberalism concentrates on the rights of the tolerated. He further claims that Locke emphasizes the alleged irrationality of persecution, but is silent as to its immorality. In brief, where modern philosophy concentrates on the tolerated, Locke concentrates on the tolerators, and where modern philosophy concentrates on morality, Locke concentrates on rationality (Waldron 1988: 61–86). These two contrasts between Locke and modern liberals highlight the fact that Locke's justification of toleration has virtually nothing to say either about individual self-development or about truth. The two major modern grounds for toleration are grounds to which Locke never refers.

In what follows I shall discuss a Lockean account of toleration and suggest that it contains some important considerations which should be incorporated in any modern discussion of toleration. When they are incorporated, we will, I believe, have a better understanding of the three forms of silence mentioned above.

III

Locke on truth and toleration

In his account of the wrong done by religious persecution Locke concedes that there is a truth, and that there may be a weighty interest in discovering that truth. Nevertheless, the important question is not a question about truth, but about the legitimate, and rational, use of state power. He makes reference not only to what it is proper for the state to do (this is a familiar liberal theme), but also to what can be achieved by state power – what authorities can rationally aim at.

Thus Locke argues in the case of religious toleration that the means available to the state are simply inadequate to achieve religious conformity. 'It is only light and evidence that can work a change in men's opinions', he declares (1956: 130), and these cannot be attained via the coercive means at the disposal of the state. The general theme is not simply of what government may *legitimately* attempt to do, but of what government can *actually* achieve.

This aspect of Locke's account of toleration has come under attack from a variety of commentators; specifically, it has been argued that, although correct in his claim that belief is not subject to the will, Locke is naive to suppose that pressure cannot be brought to bear on the 'epistemic apparatus' which surrounds belief. For sure, magistrates cannot, by use of coercion, compel people to believe. Nevertheless, they can manipulate and control the information available to the public in such a way as to mould and inform belief. Thus Jeremy Waldron says:

> Suppose the religious authorities know that there are certain books that would be sufficient, if read, to shake the faith of an otherwise orthodox population. Then, although again people's beliefs cannot be controlled directly by coercive means, those who wield political power can put it to work indirectly to reinforce belief by banning everyone on pain of death from reading or obtaining copies of these heretical tomes. Such means may well be efficacious even though they are intolerant and oppressive. (Waldron 1988: 81)

But again, Locke's point is not so much a point about what government may attempt by means of coercion, but about what such coercion actually achieves. In particular, it is Locke's claim that in the religious case coercion cannot achieve the right kind of assent. It may elicit verbal assent, but it cannot elicit genuine belief. Moreover, even if we suppose that the kind of indirect coercion alluded to by Waldron would be sufficient to secure sincere belief, this sincerity is, in Locke's eyes, distinct from authenticity, and authenticity is what is required for salvation (light is needed to change men's opinions).

The distinction between sincerity and authenticity may be clarified by considering Bernard Williams's discussion of the nature of belief. In his article 'Deciding to believe' Williams (1973) points to four conditions which are necessary for authentic belief. Amongst these is what he calls the 'acceptance' condition. This condition dictates that for full blown belief we need both the possibility of deliberate reticence (not saying what I believe) and the possibility of insincerity (saying something other than what I believe). The point of the acceptance condition is to indicate that sincere utterance is neither a necessary nor a sufficient condition of belief: not necessary because we may choose to be reticent about our beliefs; not sufficient because the possibility of insincere utterance must be available to the speaker if it is to be appropriate to refer to him as a believer. Depending on how certain beliefs are induced, it may be that the acceptance condition goes unsatisfied. Cases of hypnotism might be of this sort, as might cases of brainwashing. When people have been hypnotized or subjected to brainwashing they are (characteristically) unable to say anything other than what they have been induced to say. Of course, the scenario which Waldron envisages in which belief is indirectly coerced will not be of this dramatic sort, but such cases do nevertheless serve to cast doubt on the general assumption that all that is required for authentic belief is sincere utterance plus a causal story.

The point of these considerations is not to cast doubt on the claim that coercion may work on the epistemic apparatus which surrounds belief. It is simply to resist the move from that claim to the claim that authentic belief is constituted only by sincere utterance plus a causal story. In claiming that light is needed to change men's opinions Locke is pointing to an important difficulty in the philosophy of mind, and one which has consequences for moral and political philosophy. This is, quite simply, that even though magistrates, judges, accusers, may indeed extract confession, and may extract sincere confession, that is not necessarily enough, for there is a morally significant gap between authenticity and sincerity. In the religious case, more than simple sincerity is required. And the same may be true, I believe, for cases other than the religious case.[1]

It seems to me that Locke's defence of religious toleration may be extended to apply to the First and Fifth Amendment silences. I hope also that extending it in this way will help to explain further the distinction between sincerity and authenticity, and to give greater plausibility to the Lockean account. We saw earlier that a distinction was drawn between appeals to the First Amendment and appeals to the Fifth Amendment on the grounds that the latter, but not the former, involve suppression of information. Where information was at stake it was held that the right to silence was far harder to justify, since there is often a weighty public interest in obtaining information. Locke's account of toleration, however, is indifferent as to whether there is a truth to be obtained or not. As a convinced Puritan, Locke was in no doubt that there were truths in the area of religious conviction. Nevertheless, he did not appeal to those truths as any part of his defence of toleration (nor indeed as any justification for limiting toleration). If therefore we adopt a Lockean account, the fact that there is a truth to be obtained does not, in itself, render Fifth Amendment silences different from First Amendment silences. (This, of course, is not to argue that there are no cases in which the interests of truth will be relevant. It is only to point to the fact that there are some justifications of toleration which are indifferent as to whether there is a fact of the matter or whether there is not.)

Locke's argument rests on the ownership of conscience and on the impossibility of handing over conscience to a magistrate or civil authority. It rests, in other words, on the need for authentic belief, where authentic belief cannot be obtained by coercion or manipulation. Such an argument might well extend beyond the religious case to provide the ground both for First Amendment and for Fifth Amendment silences, since in both cases what is required is precisely such a handing over of conscience to the civil authority.

In an article entitled 'Privacy and self incrimination' Robert Gerstein makes reference to a parallel defence of the Fifth Amendment right against self-incrimination, arguing that 'we are dealing here with a special sort of information, a sort of information which it is particularly important for the individual to be able to control; ... the admission of wrongdoing, self condemnation, the revelation of remorse ... have generally been regarded as a matter between a man and his conscience, or his God. It is not the disclosure of the facts, but the *mea culpa*, the public admission of the private judgement of self-condemnation, that seems to be of real concern' (Gerstein 1984: 249).

The argument from conscience, or from authentic belief, is, moreover, distinct from any argument in terms of individual autonomy or self-development. In liberal political philosophy arguments from autonomy concentrate on the interest of the individual in making his own life. Notoriously, where the individual has no such interest, the argument from autonomy is threatened. This argument, by contrast, concentrates on what it is legitimate (or even possible) for a government or authority to demand. In brief, it is like Locke's argument both in its emphasis on authenticity and in its emphasis on the obligations of government rather than the rights of individuals.

Gerstein refers to it as a privacy argument, but it seems to me that the distinction between the disclosure of facts and the *mea culpa* makes this more properly an ownership argument. Handing over conscience is something which government cannot rationally demand, and there are two reasons why the demand is inappropriate: first because authenticity cannot be extracted, and second because, in demanding it, governments go beyond what they can properly attain. The two reasons are of course connected, but each reason points to a justification of toleration which is quite distinct from the justifications offered by modern liberals. The Lockean account, in so far as it concentrates on the irrationality of persecution and the obligations of magistrates, answers more closely to the wrong which is done by intolerance than do modern explanations. Moreover, it provides at least the seeds of a justification for the right to silence, and the seeds of a more general justification of civil disobedience as warranted not because opinions have been suppressed, but because governments have attempted to take upon themselves the conscience of the individual.

IV

Toleration, silence and civil disobedience

In comparing First and Fifth Amendment silences, appeal has been made to Locke's argument concerning the impossibility of handing over conscience to the state, magistrate, or civil authority. I turn now to the case for civil disobedience advanced by Russell and ask whether there is a similar point to be made here also. Earlier in the paper I referred to Russell's claim that in modern society the inequalities of power are such that it may often happen that the public lacks the information on which to reach a reasoned decision. In saying this Russell is appealing to the value of truth as both a ground for, and a limit on, toleration. However, in discussing Locke's argument I urged that truth was not the most relevant consideration in matters of toleration. What then is to be said about civil disobedience in cases such as that cited by Russell?

To recall, it is Russell's claim that civil disobedience may be justified as the only defence against massive public ignorance, or to ensure that an opinion has received a fair hearing. One difficulty with his account is that it is hard, *a priori*, to give criteria which specify when an opinion has in fact received a fair hearing. As Singer points out, there is a temptation to suppose that so long as the opinion is not accepted by the majority of people, it is an opinion which has not received a fair hearing (Singer 1973: 76). Thus, Russell himself implies that the mere fact that there is no public outcry against nuclear defence policy is itself evidence that the opinion has not been adequately presented. Russell may well be right in the specific case, but it is hard to see that this constitutes an *argument* for his position, rather than merely a statement of it.

Again, we may turn to the 'handing over of conscience' as a justification of civil disobedience. In defending free speech, reference is often made to truth and to autonomy. But increasingly (particularly in the United States) free speech is defended as a means of promoting and sustaining democracy. The most famous proponent of this line of thought is Alexander Meiklejohn, who construes the First Amendment as primarily aimed at enabling the people to understand political issues and thus to participate effectively in the workings of democracy. As Barendt points out, one awkwardness with this defence is that it renders problematic the suppression of opinion by the majority acting through its elected representatives. He asks, 'If the maintenance of democracy is the foundation for free speech, how is one to argue against the regulation or suppression of that speech by the democracy acting through its elected representatives?' (Barendt 1985: 21).

The answer is in part given by reference to the handing over of conscience. It is not, as Barendt suggests, the possibility of criticism of government, or the possibility of political change alone which are the objects of a free speech provision, but the fact that, in a democracy, governments act in our name. Within a democracy we do, to an extent, hand over conscience. Furthermore, in so doing we create inequalities of power which themselves render safeguards necessary. Again, this argument is distinct from the argument from autonomy: the autonomy argument supposes that people are interested in participating in political decisions. It supposes 'active' citizenship. The argument from conscience, however, does not suppose that all (or even most) citizens are active in this way. It simply recognizes that there has been a handing over of conscience and specifies limits to that transference.

However, defences of civil disobedience in terms of conscience have recently fallen into disrepute. Thus, for example, Peter Singer argues that those who appeal to conscience display a fundamental misunderstanding of the nature of democracy.

> Those who think they must disobey democratic laws in order to avoid acquiescing, or seeming to acquiesce, in particular results of the democratic system are mistaken: their actions are really indicative of a refusal to acquiesce in the democratic system itself. (Singer 1973: 104)

This line of thinking concedes (in principle at least) the legitimacy of refusing to be associated with acts which are held to be immoral. Specifically, it recognizes the objections an individual may have to 'handing over conscience' in circumstances where that will implicate him in acts he believes to be morally wrong. The response, however, is that it is a misunderstanding of the nature of democracy to suppose that acquiescence (or apparent acquiescence) is the only alternative to disobedience. The individual who protests loudly, but stops short of civil disobedience, cannot be construed as acquiescing in the objectionable government policy. At most, he is acquiescing in democracy. By contrast, the individual who engages in civil disobedience is, in some circumstances, refusing to acquiesce in the democratic system itself which is, in Singer's view, a procedure for resolving disputes. On Singer's account, therefore, civil disobedience on grounds of conscience is unjustifiable. It is a way of evincing contempt for democratic decision procedures.

There is an interesting comparison to be drawn between this account of conscience and the account offered by Kant in his discussion of the duty not to resist the sovereign. Standardly, commentators have interpreted Kant as claiming that there is no right of resistance and that disobedience is unthinkable, no matter how despotic or unjust the sovereign may be. Yet such a commitment to the authority of the sovereign fits ill with Kant's moral philosophy. As one commentator has put it, 'It is disappointing to see Kant, who champions so strongly individual autonomy in his *Grundlegung*, putting the law so emphatically above individual conscience in this respect' (Williams 1983: 204). On the surface, at least, Singer's explanation pays homage to the importance of conscience, but simply denies that civil obedience is tantamount to offering up conscience. By contrast, Kant appears to insist that, where the alternative is resistance to the sovereign, conscience must be offered up. But these superficial appearances are deceptive; on inspection, we can see that Kant is in fact drawing a distinction which turns Singer's account on its head. Specifically, he argues that there is a right – indeed a duty – to disobey the sovereign who commands that which is morally wrong:

> The proposition 'One must obey God rather than man' means only that if the latter commands something which is in itself evil (immediately opposed to the moral law), it may not and ought not to be obeyed. . . .
>   If it is said 'One ought to obey God rather than man' it means nothing but this: if statutory commands in regard to what men can legislate and judge come into conflict with duties which reason unconditionally prescribes, and concerning whose fulfilling or trespassing God alone can be a judge, then the former yield authority to the latter. (Kant 1922–3: vi 244, 302–3)

In brief, we may draw a distinction between the right of resistance and the right to disobey, where the Kantian prohibition on the former is not thereby a prohibition on the latter. Hancock discusses this distinction with specific reference to the possibility of communication between members of a society. On his interpretation Kant's claim is that 'no actually functioning government can justifiably command and expect obedience from its subjects unless there is, as a minimum, free communication in some sense between the individual members of a political society and those who exercise the authority by which they are governed' (Hancock 1975: 173). It is, therefore, the possibility of communication, not the pursuit of truth, which justifies civil disobedience. In 'What is Orientation in Thinking?' Kant says:

> One can well say that the external power which wrests from man the freedom publicly to communicate his thoughts also takes away his freedom to think – the sole jewel that remains to us under all civil repression and through which alone counsel against the evils of the state can be undertaken. (Kant 1949: 303)

This defence is distinct from a defence of toleration as necessary in order to expose lies and falsehoods. For Kant, toleration does not aim at truth, rather it is one of the conditions necessary for thinking. Like Russell, therefore, he insists on public communication, and his assertion that this is necessary in order to guard against 'the evils of the state' sounds like Russell's claim that publicity is necessary in order to expose the lies of the

Establishment. But for Kant, toleration does not aim at truth, it is the precondition of thought. Thus, on Russell's account, the evil against which toleration operates, and which justifies civil disobedience, is the evil of thinking what is false. For Kant, by contrast, the evil is the destruction of thought itself. Again, it is the handing over of conscience which is to be avoided.

V

Conclusion

The specific aim of this paper has been to discuss three forms of silence and their significance to questions of toleration. More generally, I have been critical of standard liberal defences of toleration in terms of truth and autonomy, and have suggested that such defences fail to answer to the wrong which is done by intolerance. The Lockean argument, expressed in terms of authentic belief, explains what is wrong with removing the privilege against self-incrimination – or at least gives some reasons for doubting that a weighty public interest in the truth is sufficient to justify intolerance. Similar doubts as to whether toleration is justified in terms of truth arise via a consideration of Kant's discussion of the duty never to resist the sovereign: toleration is not to be explained by reference to truth, but neither is it a matter of individual moral purity. Information is not what toleration aims at, but what is presupposed by it. Thus, the justification of disobedience is not that disobedience is the only way of asserting truth, but that disobedience is necessary in order to think for oneself.

A final point: to claim that toleration is necessary in order to think for oneself is not to claim that it is necessary for the development of individual autonomy. In modern political philosophy, 'autonomy' tends to refer to the agent's capacity to lead his own life, or pursue his own conception of the good independent of government interference. By contrast, both Locke and Kant have a more restricted, yet also a more profound conception of what is involved in thinking for oneself. Modern liberals are characteristically committed to the claim that conceptions of the good life are 'a matter of opinion', that they are proper objects of individual choice, and that they are the business only of the individual himself. Neither Kant nor Locke share this commitment to the optional. For Locke, there are religious truths, and it matters that men come to know them. For Kant, there are requirements of reason, and again it matters that men operate within them. But not any way of accepting truth, or conforming to reason will suffice. Both believe that there are distinct limits to what can legitimately be 'handed over'. For Locke, of course, these limits are provided by consideration of what is needed for salvation, but Kant too insists that not everything can be handed over. He says;

> It is so convenient! If I have a book to have understanding in place of me, a spiritual adviser to have a conscience in place of me, a doctor to judge my diet for me and so on, I need not make any effort at all. (Kant, 'What is Enlightenment?' in 1970: 54)

The crucial concept here is that of *effort* – as opposed to choice. It is not, in Kant's view, my right to choose what I shall think. Rather, it is my duty to employ reason in my thinking – to retain command over my conscience, however convenient the alternative might be. Again, there is a sense in which the attempt, via intolerance, to deny people the possibility of thinking for themselves is ultimately doomed to failure, and this is not because individuals have a right to make choices for themselves, but because they have a duty to think for themselves.

In democratic societies, the sounds of silence may be as significant as the sounds of speech: what we don't hear, or won't say is as important as what we do hear, and what we do say. The intolerance which is evinced in the erosion of the privilege against self-incrimination is most easily excused if we suppose that toleration is justified by reference to truth. Locke gives us reason to doubt whether that justification is adequate. This doubt, however, poses a problem for defences of civil disobedience as warranted when an opinion is not receiving a fair hearing. For here it may appear that such action can be legitimated only by reference to the need to know. But the Kantian and Lockean accounts provide an alternative explanation – the need to know is of secondary importance; it is the duty to understand which is primary, and that duty can be fulfilled only in a society where silence is understood as itself a form of communication, which is just as important as speech.

Note

1.   The textual evidence for this interpretation of Locke's *Letter* is discussed in greater detail in Mendus 1989: ch. 2.

PART III
Power

9. Anarchists against the Revolution

Stephen Clark

I

Taking anarchism seriously

The popular image of an anarchist is such that it may seem wilfully paradoxical to suggest that any sort of anarchist is against any sort of revolution. Anarchists are supposed to be old-fashioned nihilists and random revolutionaries, who hold that power grows out of the mouth of a gun and aim to terrorize conventional and law-abiding society into submission to their own half-baked schemes. Only their supposed inefficiency saves them from being the most hated of terrorists, for whereas other such military groups aim (however foolishly or wickedly) at the restoration of civil peace and orderly justice after a dishonourable peace and systematic injustice have been dismantled, anarchistical revolutionaries are supposed to have no further ideas about 'what comes after' the downfall of established order. Mere destruction is their *métier*.

That there are some such people I would not presume to deny, nor that they sometimes call themselves 'anarchists' . But three things need to be made clear from the start. First, the rejection of all authority that is attributed to anarchists is actually the professed doctrine of a good many modernist political philosophers. If I have no obligations at all save those to which I myself freely consent (which is to say, if nothing is sacred) then I have no obligation to obey at any rate my own government (though, paradoxically, I might owe such an obligation to the governments of those countries I choose to visit), nor any duties either of care or forbearance to any but my freely chosen friends – and even those duties must be renewed from moment to moment if they are to remain real. Secondly, while only some anarchists have advocated military violence to overthrow the state, all modern 'archists' countenance such violence to maintain the state. Thirdly, anarchists do generally acknowledge an 'unchosen authority'.

Anarchy, as the desired form of society, is not lack of *order* (which would, etymologically, be *ataxia*) nor even of authority or law, but lack of *government*, of a ruling class or caste or office distinct from ordinary members of society. Anarchists, it has often been said, are unafraid Jeffersonian democrats convinced, with Thomas Paine, that

> the great part of that order which reigns among mankind is not the effect of government. It has its origins in the principles of society and the natural constitution of men.... Common interest regulates their concerns and forms their laws; and the laws which common usage ordains, have a greater influence than the laws of government. (Paine 1792: 1; see Ostergaard 1981: 183)

What those common laws and interests exactly are is, of course, a matter of some debate. Paine himself is usually associated with the Enlightenment rejection of merely local norms and customs, and that rationalism has played a part in subsequent anarchist theory. But another strand of anarchism has instead opposed the rationalist tradition, seeing that it invariably ends up as the tool of despots eager to destroy the hard-won liberties and values of the people. On which subject I will have more to say below.

Modern 'archists' attempt to think of nation-states and their centralizing governments as the free creation of cooperating individuals. Older, or more conservative, archists saw them as the proper expression and embodiment of moral value. 'The pre nineteenth century state did not serve nations; it did not even serve communities. It served God, the Heavenly Mandate, the Law of Allah' (Navari 1981: 13). This aphorism somewhat exaggerates the number of divinely mandated governments, but it is fair to say that those governments which did claim such a mandate had at least a much more limited role in society than modern politicians claim with less excuse. Anarchists tend to think of governments as the heirs of robber lords, more or less humanized. All governing elites have either seized power by military force, or inherit powers first seized by military force, or retain powers first conceded to them so as to organize resistance to military force. In days gone by, whether in Rome or Israel, war-leaders were nominated by acclamation, for the duration of the defence, and then went home to their farms and businesses. Now governments and their associated schoolmen relish the thought that the spirit evoked in present danger may be carried over into the 'peace'. Such a national purpose, of course, is not well liked by modernists when it leads the population to resist the rational order that they prefer. Its absence, as people revert to living in families, clubs, churches, craft-guilds and neighbourhoods, is liked even less. According to Kropotkin, the law's origin is the desire of the ruling class to give permanence to customs imposed by themselves for their own advantage. Its character is the skilful commingling of customs useful to society, customs which have no need of law to ensure respect, with other customs useful only to rulers, injurious to the mass of the people and maintained only by the fear of punishment. (Kropotkin 1976: 34)

But of course that quotation may give substance to the suspicion that anarchists are a little naive. Even if people were convinced that anarchists did not love disorder and destruction they would insist that what anarchists confessedly desire – the end of government – would actually lead to disorder and widespread destruction, or else to the entrenchment of local customs of a thoroughly bad kind. The present condition of the Lebanon reveals one danger; rules of non-interference between nation-states, which exist within an international 'anarchical' society (see Bull 1977), and are thus enabled to deal iniquitously with their subjects, reveal another. 'Government' (which is to say, oppression) may appear at any level of social organization, from patriarchal household to commune to village to slave-owning confederacy, and the next higher level of organization may intervene to *save* the oppressed even if it also engages in oppression. Giving up state-government may merely legitimate older forms of tyranny. It may be true, in Mazor's words, that 'there is more to be feared from a malefactor armed with law, a court, a police force, or an army than from the same person limited to the use of bare hands' (Mazor 1978: 155) but domestic tyrants, village patriarchs, charismatic cult-leaders (all of whom might relish the absence of the state) have more than their bare hands to use. It is one thing to agree that 'although law has been depicted as the great equalizer, more often it serves as the means of multiplying advantage' (Mazor 1978: 152); quite another to resolve the problem by abolishing the law.

In short, the anarchists' historically accurate account of how state-governments emerge, and their reasonable disinclination to give any present government much moral credit, cannot be taken seriously as a reason for rejecting state-law unless they have something to say about how we might instead preserve a decent civil peace. Actually, they do, and despite the many and expectable disagreements between different schools and traditions, there are also real, and deep, agreements: all distinguish between the military and the civil means, sometimes calling the former 'the political' and the latter 'the economic' means.

II

Understandings of the civil means

It is possible, or at least imaginable, that there are forms of human life such that every adult human being can make or obtain everything she needs without needing to deal with any other human. Such a person, Aristotle thought, must either be a wild beast or a god (*Politics,* I, 1153a29). Certainly her life can be of little immediate interest to us. All of *us* need many things that only other people can supply, from food, shelter, clothing and companionship to transport, books, computers and health care. Once we are in this situation we can obtain what we need in only two ways, by 'voluntary' or 'involuntary' transaction (Aristotle 1908–52:*Nicomachean Ethics*, V, 1131alff.). In other words we must either take them from an unwilling producer, or accept them from a willing donor. If we choose the path of coercion we shall in the end require an army (literally) of helpers who will 'persuade' producers to 'give' us the goods. Brigands and hunters alike are predators, but those who would hunt humans will quickly find that the prey can be very dangerous. Just as hunters can become pastoralists or farmers (while their prey accepts an increasingly rigid control of their movements, feeding and reproduction) (see Ingold 1974: 523ff.), so brigands may become feudal lords and governors. If a king claims to be 'Shepherd of the People', it is worth recalling what shepherds want from sheep. Such lords have never yet succeeded, unlike farmers, in breeding a docile subject population, though they have sought to do so by enlisting those of the subject population who might otherwise oppose them into their own ranks. My own suspicion is that even a rigorously enforced breeding and selection programme never completely works – though it has come very close to doing so, and there are some societies where dissent seems to have been fairly thoroughly dampened. When this has (almost) happened even the masters seem like slaves. But most governors, unlike farmers, still need to coerce unwilling subjects with the sword, or bribe them with the heady delights of power, or cause them to believe that the *government* is owed the loyalty that is often given to a nation or fellowship.

But there was always an alternative, namely to rely on voluntary transactions. Economic exchange begins in mutual gift-giving: if I have more pumpkins than I know what to do with, and you are similarly endowed with beetroot, we may both stand to gain by a swap. Neither of us needs to be coerced. Such face-to-face transactions between friends (or friends of friends) can even be spread out over time. I may 'give' on the assumption that you will 'give' in return. I may even 'give' without expecting a direct return from you, so long as there are enough gifts floating in the system that I do stand to gain by continuing the flow. Grasping accumulation of what I can neither use nor choose to give away is an anomaly: either the supply of gifts will dry up, or some mechanism is introduced to free the jam. Accumulators, in 'non-civilized' societies, have periodic feasts or massive gift-giving sessions or pot-smashing ceremonies to restore the flow (see Sahlins 1972). Even very distant communities, say on a scattered island chain, may be united by the passage of ceremonial 'gifts' along the line.

Aristotle – as Karl Polanyi has pointed out (1957) – was close enough to the origins of strictly economic exchange to see how it might be (and was being) perverted by the invention of markets, middle men, and money, when 'wealth accumulates and men decay'. It is at this point that the various schools of anarchism begin to divide, though all retain the idea that 'voluntary transaction' is the only permissible kind of acquisition from another.

Anarcho-communists (which is what most people now understand by 'anarchists') look back to the experience of family, village and, generally, 'gift-giving' life, maintained by a sense of kinship and long-term advantage. In the absence of a centralized authority with a monopoly of military force, people would and should subside into naturally occurring communes, cantons, ceremonial chains. Such local or occasionally emergent groups would make the necessary decisions by the free exchange of ideas and gifts. The general preference would be for genuinely consensus decisions, reached over a lengthy exploratory process. 'The non-western political pattern of decision-making,' Burton says, 'is an intensive and time-taking consultative process in which different views are argued until consensus emerges, and this is confirmed in a final vote' (1968: 23). I share enough of the Western 'social construction of reality' to suspect that such a 'consensus' is actually often only the product of power-politics, but there is certainly something to be said for a nonadversarial style of management.

Anarcho-communists also tend to object to 'private property', the notion that any of us can have an absolute right to use, destroy, embellish, exchange, or limit others' use of anything whatsoever, having no regard to the common wealth and interest of our manifold societies. In Proudhon's words, 'property is theft'. The first person to put a marker on a piece of land or ancestral mathom and say 'this is *mine*' was the first owner of capital, the first thief, the first magician. In anarcho-communist utopias people keep things as long as it is their turn to use them, and greet with incomprehension the suggestion that anything could 'belong' to anyone in particular: does the sunlight? 'The earth is given as a common stock for man to labor and live on' (Thomas Jefferson in Koch 1961: 28), and no one can dictate the terms on which any portion of that common inheritance is to be used.

Anarcho-capitalists (or libertarians), on the other hand, found their case precisely upon 'private property'. In Proudhon's words, 'property is liberty'. The first person to work a piece of land by planting and gardening it so 'mixed her labor' with it that it was 'hers'. Individuals can only be genuinely free, and free of coercive power, if they are protected in the cultivation and enjoyment of their own. If what I make can be taken from me, with general approval, then my powers are not my own: I am as much a slave as I would be if admitted brigands treated me as prey. Private property and the commercial spirit are always being denounced by would-be despots, who pretend that we would all be happier if we knew our place. Where there is no room for me to work by and for myself my 'liberty' is nugatory. A genuinely free society must therefore make it possible for all of us to have and keep 'our own'. Unfree societies rest on the pretence of giving the citizen a chance to share in collective decision-making, but take from her effective control over what most immediately concerns her. Like Herbert Spencer's slave , she is induced to accept her lot by the appearance of a chance to share the dangerous delights of telling others what to do though nothing that she individually says ever makes any difference (Spencer 1969; see Clark 1985). In anarcho-capitalist utopias every individual has an absolute authority over her own body and the products of her will – saving only that she concedes an equal liberty to all – and greets the suggestion that anyone else should rule her with incomprehension. 'It is said', said Jefferson, 'that men are not able to govern themselves: have we found angels in the shape of kings to govern them?' If human beings cannot rule themselves, how can they rule others? 'The true foundation of republican government is the equal right of every citizen, in his person and property' (Koch 1961: 28).

Put like this it may seem obvious that 'anarchists' and 'libertarians' are radically different breeds, united only in their dislike of current arrangements and a wish to 'run their own lives' whether as individuals or as communards. There are certainly deepseated differences of temperament at work, easily revealed through a simple thought experiment. Suppose some children are squabbling over a flute, and you are the only adult around. One child made the flute; another is the best flute-player; a third is lonely and depressed and would get enormous pleasure from possessing the thing; and a fourth is the strongest of the group. What (if anything) do you do? Right-thinking liberal parents of my acquaintance generally reply that they would confiscate the flute, and then return it with an instruction that it must be shared. Social Darwinists, I suppose, must let the fourth child have it. Speaking personally, I think the maker should be helped to repossess it, even if one adds a gentle encouragement to sharing or to renting it out for hire. Others again suggest that everyone gets together to learn how to make flutes. There are distinct differences, in short, between the degree of authority that adults claim, the criteria by which they assess desert and the ideal form of relationship they seek to inculcate. Those differences identify some adults as certainly not anarchists of either type, but even the anarchically inclined may regard each other with suspicion. Anarchists and libertarians regularly read each other out of the tradition, but 'the differences between individualist and socialist anarchism, though important, should not be exaggerated' (Ostergaard 1981: 183). Witness the following quotations:

1. Each individual, each association, commune or province, each region and nation has the absolute right to determine its own fate, to associate with others or not, to ally itself with whoever it will, or break any alliance, without regard to so-called historical claims or the convenience of its neighbors.[1]

2. It is by dividing and subdividing the republics from the National One down thro' all its subordinations, until it ends in the administration of every man's farm and affairs by himself; by placing under everyone what his own eye may superintend, that all will be done for the best.[2]

The first is from Bakunin, anarcho-communist and revolutionary, who thereby espoused as extreme a rejection of the laws of contract and historical association as any modern individualist, while emphasizing the importance of putting power in the hands of those who suffer its effects. The second is from Thomas Jefferson, and a reminder that Proudhon, who accepted the title 'anarchist,' actually played with the idea of saying 'federalist' (by which he meant Jeffersonian, not Hamiltonian) instead. He was perhaps put off by the appropriation of that term by the founders of federal power in the United States. 'I had rather', said one opponent of the new US Constitution in 1787, 'be a free citizen of the small republic of Massachusetts than an oppressed subject of the great American empire' (Borden 1965: 2). A proper federalism allows and protects the unfettered emergence of consensus and dissent at all levels. On the one side Kropotkin, most sympathetic and intelligent of anarcho-communists, denounced what he called 'state-capitalism' and 'collectivism' as tending to demoralize and dehumanize the recipient of bureaucratic 'charity' (Kropotkin 1976: 106f.). On the other Lysander Spooner, who founded his doctrine on individual natural right, denounced government precisely for the damage it did to the land: 'it is by the monopoly of land, and the monopoly of money, that more than a thousand millions of the earth's inhabitants – as savages, barbarians and wage laborers – are kept in a state of destitution, or on the verge of destitution' (Spooner 1972: 47). It is a constant theme amongst libertarians that existing 'pro-poor' legislation actually serves the middle classes.

The difference between the two sorts of anarchist mostly turn upon their understanding of the proper civil means, and of personal freedom. Libertarians emphasize the freedom that 'money in your pocket' gives, the chance of surviving among strangers whom one does not want to owe, nor yet to own as friends. Money makes all social exchanges 'clean', uncluttered by emotional blackmail, unpaid debts or any uncertainties about what is due. Payment need not literally be made in cash, but all transactions should aim to leave 'the books balanced'. Anarcho-communists have remembered more clearly that not all human relationships are clear and external ones. And what is the point of being free if there is nothing I can actually do? Swaraj requires the eradication of poverty: positive, not only negative, freedom (Gandhi, in Jesudasan 1984). And however 'clean' the cash transactions may be, they speedily become instruments of oppression in their own right, as 'wealth accumulates' and people learn to sell what they had hitherto regarded as their own inalienable being, to be shared with friends, not handed out to strangers. There is no cash sum by which I could buy off my wife's or my children's just claims on me, even if the courts invent one.

Contrariwise, the constant appeal to 'human feeling', 'sympathy' and social identity can become as a great a barrier to freedom as any brigand's gun. As Kamienski pointed out in 1854 (*sic*) the Russian village commune was based on serfdom and was peculiarly helpful to autocracy (Walicki 1982: 192). I have similar reservations about Gandhi's proposal for federated villages and cantons in which each 'individual is always ready to perish for the village, the latter ready to perish for the circle of villages' (Jesudasan 1984: 125), and everyone restricts her desires to the range of what is currently available. This ideal is of course very *like* Jefferson's, but Jefferson had a much stronger conception of personal autonomy than Gandhi seems to have been prepared to grant. It is not easy to maintain the necessary blend of sociality and liberality that defines the free citizen:

people can be induced to 'choose' all manner of oppressive options. Government by consensus can often amount to gang rule, even to gang rape.

In sum: 'Far from being a speculative vision of a future society, anarchist society is a description of mode of organization, rooted in the experience of everyday life, which operates side by side with, and in spite of, the deviant authoritarian trend of our society' (Ward 1973: 14). But that mode may either be the normal familial one, or else the normal economic one, modelled on unlimited and friendly sharing or else on definite and quantifiable exchange. Both are probably necessary; either may go appallingly astray; neither should be blamed for all the evils of Soviet Russia or the Capitalist West. 'True communism was never attempted in Russia, unless one considers thirty-three categories of pay, different food rations, privileges to some and indifference to the great mass Communism.' (E. Goldman in Krimmerman and Perry 1966: 103). And Capitalism is an unknown, untried ideal (Rand 1967: 32).

III

Matters of high concern

According to one opponent of the new US Constitution, and especially of its standing army, 'it is much too early to set down for a fact that mankind cannot be governed except by Force' (1787; Borden 1965: 77). The anarchist tradition, as I have sketched it, is an expression of that conviction: mankind can be governed – or rather mankind, through multiple free exchanges and friendly associations, can in effect govern itself – without military intervention. The order thus emerging may not be one that any mortal being had in mind before: it is not imposed *a priori* on a struggling mass, but grows out of the unfettered, unforced life of humanity. Once the actual and imagined brigands have been swept aside the 'organization of the civil or economic means' will operate in peace. Unfortunately, the brigands show no sign of being swept aside, and even 'opponents of big government' always seem to leave office having extended the power of central government into yet further regions and cut back not at all on its previous claims. Rudyard Kipling, in his only extant works of what came to be called 'science fiction' (1917), imagines a future where the single, limited global authority has only the task of keeping the lines of transport and communication open, and everyone else has retreated to the eminently proper task of minding her own business. In this world the idea of letting your actions be decided by majority vote or by obedience to dictatorial whim are alike insane. A mixture of clan loyalty and commercial exchange serves well enough to keep the peace.

But Kipling did put that future on the far side of a global war, culminating in the desperate revolt commemorated in 'MacDonough's Song' (Kipling 1917):

> Whether the State can loose and bind
> in Heaven as well as on Earth;
> if it be wiser to kill mankind
> before or after the birth –
> these are matters of high concern
> where state-kept schoolmen are;
> but Holy State (we have lived to learn)
> endeth in Holy War.
>
> Whether the People be led by the Lord
> or lured by the loudest throat:
> if it be quicker to die by the sword
> or cheaper to die by vote –
> these are the things we have dealt with once,
> (and they will not rise from their grave)
> for Holy People, however it runs,
> endeth in wholly Slave.
>
> Whatsoever, for any cause,
> seeketh to take or give,
> power above or beyond the Laws,
> suffer it not to live!
> Holy State or Holy King –
> or Holy People's Will –
> have no truck with the senseless thing.
> Order the guns and kill!
>
> Saying after me:
> Once there was the People – Terror gave it birth!
> Once there was the People and it made a Hell of Earth!
> Once there was the People – Listen, o ye slain –
> Once there was the People: it shall never be again!

That fierce rejection of the claims of a notional, oppressive, national or other unity is, of course, of a piece with Kipling's denunciation of 'the old King, under any name', and the Law to which he refers is that battery of guarded liberties 'wrenched, inch and ell and all, slowly from the King', and by no gentle means.

So is the anarchist's only hope to organize a grand revolt against brigands, and against brigandage? Or else at least to get the revolutionary cells ready for the grand revolt that 'surely' must erupt as the contradictions of imperial power grow more unbearable? All attempts to rule by mere force require increasing effort as hostility and suspicion grow: empires collapse because so much manpower is diverted from productive life into the governmental services. The temporary solution of past empires, to conciliate the masses with free services stolen from outsiders and enlist those most likely to rebel into the hierarchy, was easier when the empires were smaller, when there was an 'outside' to ravage and when they could leave most of ordinary civil life untouched. Nowadays governments have taken on enormous responsibilities, abandoned any claim to rule by right of high moral purpose or divine mandate, cannot indefinitely push their costs onto 'the Third World' and can neither rule by fear nor rule without it. Tax evasion and the black economy swell, and government makes itself indispensable by summoning our fears of enemies across the borders. 'Whoever says State, says a State, and affirms by that the existence of several States, and whoever says several States, says: competition, jealousy, timeless and endless war' (Bakunin, in Krimmerman and Perry 1966: 84). War is the health of the State, but also its destruction.

The poet Yeats was deeply, and not unreasonably, troubled by the thoughts that words of his had encouraged into armed rebellion young Irish men who were then executed. I have no wish at all to share that kind of guilt, and luckily I do not think I need – partly, of course, because I am not a great poet!

> Mr. Jefferson said that if a centralization of power were ever effected at Washington, the US would have the most corrupt government on earth. Comparisons are difficult, but I believe it has one that is thoroughly corrupt, flagitious, tyrannical, oppressive. Yet if it were in my power to pull down its structure overnight and set up another of my own devising – to abolish the State out of hand, and replace it by an organization of the economic means – I would not do it, for the minds of Americans are far from fitted to any such great change as this, and the effect would be only to lay open the way for the worse enormities of usurpation – possibly, who knows, with myself as the usurper! (A.J. Nock, 'Anarchist's progress', in Buckley 1970: 143)

What Jefferson, Yeats and Nock all praise and look to under different names is the common, custom-led civilities of ordinary life. What all oppose is the imposition of a 'rational order' decided upon by a self-styled elite. It is because Nock rejects that kind of imposition that he also rejects

Power

even the fantasy of a new revolutionary order, the temptation that Tolkien symbolized in the 'One Ring to rule them all'.

> Reason and experience alike tell us that the governments now existing in the world were established by bayonet-point, by force. None of the monarchies or governments that we see in the world are based on justice or on a correct foundation that is acceptable to reason. Their foundations are rotten, being nothing but coercion and force.[3]

Right on: but when I point out that this is a quotation from the Ayatollah Khomeini, one can be forgiven for being doubtful about the value even of a relatively bloodless revolution (as was Iran's) and the imposition of a truly 'rational' order. 'The ills of rebellion are certain, but the event doubtful', as Berkeley advised the potential rebels of an earlier day (Berkeley 1948: VI 55). Even if a car is being very badly driven it is usually madness for a passenger to wrench the wheel away, and not necessarily much benefit to other passengers if she succeeds.

People who believe that there is a rationally discernible 'right' order suppose that anyone who would have any view on the matter will reach the same, correct result unless they are deceived by vanity and false philosophy. It is unusual to remember that one might oneself be in that dire position. Rationalists are therefore usually indistinguishable from dogmatists: what I believe is both correct and the only really rational opinion, and I need pay no heed – indeed I should not pay such heed – to any unreasonable person who, influenced by superstition and immediate passion, does not think the same. It hardly matters whether such rationalists admire a God made in their image, Humanity or Reason or the Self itself. Their objection to an actual government will only be an objection to that transient government, and not to the very principle of institutional control, mobilized against the enemies of rational order. Notoriously, Randian 'objectivism' leads on to as fierce a contempt for 'altruists' and 'non-objectivists' as ever Khomeini showed for nationalists or corrupt Westerners. David Friedman (1978: 204) cites H.L.Mencken: 'After a revolution the successful revolutionists always try to convince doubters that they have achieved great things and usually they hang any man who denies it.'

Non-coercive anarchism (which is to say, just anarchism) rests instead upon a method of civil association, not on a perceived goal. That method, the organization of the civil means, has no one obvious outcome, and to that extent the critics are correct to see that anarchists have no definite political goal, 'no good society' the far side of catastrophe. Certain possible futures are rejected (as imperial consolidation, bureaucratic world state, military nationalism), but the anarchist methodology is compatible with as many more, including the free market, communitarian federalism and even 'fractured feudalism' (an idealized version of the medieval European experiment, where the existence of many structures of authority precluded any absolute control by priest or baron).

IV

The rules of war

That final possibility – of a civil order that emerges to contain the brigands without recourse to some yet stronger brigand – allows me to introduce the rules developed in that medieval period for the conduct of war. These rules – however ill-observed they have been in this century – still constitute our strongest evidence of an international, anarchical authority. Two sources of their power in the medieval period can be identified: the threat of excommunication, and the threat from mercenary soldiers, who would not long lend their support to princes who involved them in too dangerous or unprofitable wars.

The rules of war require that war only be fought (i) on proper authority, (ii) for a just cause, (iii) with right intent, (iv) for the sake of peace, (v) when all other methods of resolving the dispute have failed, (vi) without direct injury to noncombatant, (vii) without cruel or unusual weapons, (viii) with a sense of proportion or discrimination in the means used (Johnson 1975: 72f.). In sum, a war is fought justly when it approximates to the action of a decent police force or protection agency, when it is something that people used to civil peace could cautiously endorse. Obviously the 'justice' of the cause is likely to be moot, and it has generally been identified solely with 'self-defence'. In Islamic terms: *Jihad*, war to spread the Islamic laws throughout the world, can be initiated only by an Imam, one with the clear Mandate of Heaven, whereas *Defa'*, to defend one's liberty to obey those laws, is a universal right (Rajaee 1983: 89). Plenty of people have thought they had Heaven's Mandate – including Genghis Khan (see Voegelin 1952: 57) – but it is difficult not to doubt their credentials. A just war should leave people at *liberty:* which is to say, one should not claim the right to dictate their condition. But even if we have no Imam, so just war theory says, we need an acknowledged prince to order us to war. Must this not be an element of the theory that anarchists reckon superfluous? No prince can make an action right that would not have been right anyway, for despotism exactly is 'that principle in performance of which the state arbitrarily puts into effect laws which it has itself made' (Kant, 'Perpetual Peace', in Kant 1970). Laws of the lawmaker's own making 'have no color of authority or obligation' (Spooner 1972: 3). So why might I not initiate military violence in defence of myself, my friends, my dependants, if anyone may?

But in a society ruled by emergent order, and diffused authority, any such military action runs the risk of stepping past its bounds. 'If [a police agency] commit an act of invasion against someone that someone had better turn out to deserve it, otherwise they are the criminals' (Rothbard 1982: 82). That is reason enough for me not to run the risk except in the most obvious and immediate of cases, and cause enough to ensure that I shall not have the wherewithal to do so. Who would assist me in the enterprise unless they trusted my judgement of what was a wrong, and unless they believed that I would accept responsibility if I turned out to be mistaken? How, in turn, could I accept responsibility for what my assistants did unless I could trust them not to go too far? A military action cannot be, and cannot be taken to have been, a simple aggregate of individuals' actions. It must be a campaign, a corporate act, for which responsibility must be variously assigned. Unless someone has the resources to compensate those who are unjustly injured in the fight (and even nonculpable injuries deserve some damages); unless someone has the resources to track down the injuries and the invaders that are her excuse for war; unless someone can earn the respect and voluntary obedience of her troops – there can be no proper authority for such an act, and those who nonetheless resort to violence do so at their own risk – a risk which might leave them paying restitution to their intended and accidental victims for all their natural lives. That defines the nature of a prince in an anarchical society: one who has the resources, and respect, to enlist assistants, and to pay up for their errors, and her own. Despite the precedent of Nuremberg, it is noticeable that current rulers do not accept responsibility for what they order done. It seems indeed to be accepted practice that fallen tyrants are expected to live out their lives in comfortable exile, and only their least henchmen suffer punishment (let alone make restitution for their crimes). It is the mark of a slavish nature to avoid responsibility, the mark of a slave to enslave others if she can: twice over, such tyrants are slaves.

The rules of war reveal, yet again, that existing state-authorities have no *moral* authority: they do not accept responsibility as princes should, and plan such actions as outrage the rules of war. Those leaders who unleash a nuclear war (and all their assistants) would – if the survivors managed to get hold of them – be justly tried for genocide, except that there could be no adequate revenge. But by the same token revolutionary leaders who abuse their followers' trust by organizing car-bombings, assassination of fathers before their children's eyes, necklace-murders and the like have also no good right to be considered more than brigands. From the anarchist perspective there is no intrinsic difference between a state-government and a revolutionary gang: both claim a right to deploy military force against their enemies in defence of what they mind about; both reject external claims to judgment on their doings; both tend to justify themselves either by direct reference to a divine or moral mandate, or to the more or less forced consent of 'their' people.

Just revolutions, in sum, are theoretically possible, on the same terms as just wars. But there is very strong reason to be suspicious of any candidates for that high status. Certainly neither war nor revolution can be just that does not revert as soon as possible to the civil means, to peace. Certainly the very establishment of a war machine will almost always make that return less likely. The means constitute and modify the end, as Gandhi saw. All would-be revolutionaries need to ask themselves which programme is likelier to succeed: armed revolution, with its ensuing injuries to innocents, its incitement of established brigands to yet harsher measures, its creation of another brigand power, or else some unsung, unrebellious organization of the civil and economic means alongside or out of the way of politics? Even the temptation to engage in 'nonviolent disobedience' may not really be the best idea, nor really be 'nonviolent': inciting others to violence, even against oneself, in the hope that they will gradually lose heart, is not altogether an anarchical ideal. Anarchists, in brief, will often be against the revolution precisely because they distrust the political or military means, because they see the possibility of organizing through the civil or economic means, and gradually letting the state wither. Precisely because the state has no real authority neither do most rebellions.

Notes

1. Bakunin as quoted in Geurin 1970: 67.
2. Jefferson as quoted in Koch 1943: 163.
3. A. Khomeini, Kashf Asras 221, in Rajaee 1983: 76.

10. The Civilizers versus the Barbarians: Power Relations between Centre and Periphery in Italy

Martin Bull

> You [Italians of the North] have no choice: either you succeed in making us [Italians of the South] civilized, or we shall succeed in making you barbarians.

> Pasquale Villari

I

The remit of this paper is the centre–periphery dimension of protest and power. The inclusion of such a dimension can be regarded as essential because the idea of protest or conflict is endemic to the relationship between centre and periphery, if not inherent to the conceptualization of the relationship itself. As Jean Gottmann has noted, in political geography the centre–periphery image conveys not only the idea of a 'systematic organization of space around the notion and through the function of centrality' but also 'within that established order, the opposition between the dominant centre and a subordinated periphery, suggesting the possibility of confrontation'. She adds that the political climate of this century, with its emphasis on social and political equality, 'seems to call for a restructuring of such spatial distribution as hinted at by the opposition of centre and periphery, favouring the periphery' (Gottmann 1980: 17). How is this conflictual relationship registered in practice? In what ways is it *possible* for this conflictual relationship to be registered? These are the questions which this paper addresses, and Italy is selected as a case study by which to attempt to answer them.

To those unversed in centre–periphery studies, the way in which the conflictual relationship between centre and periphery is registered may seem obvious. On the one hand, there is conflict between central government and local governments over issues relating to the autonomy – and even existence – of the latter. On the other hand, central governments in many countries experience conflict with what are often described as 'peripheral protest movements'. These movements might call for central government action for their area, they might call for regional autonomy or even for separation from the nation-state. The identification of the conflictual relationship in this manner would not be wrong. Indeed, a recent volume by Meny and Wright divides its case studies along two dimensions: 'the intergovernmental dimension' and 'the politico-spatial dimension' (Meny and Wright 1985). These two dimensions might remain separate or they might closely interrelate. Two qualifications, however, need to be made about them. First, it is often too readily assumed that there is a straightforward correlation between the intergovernmental dimension and the centre–periphery dimension itself. The existence of central and local government is often an epiphenomenon of the centre–periphery dimension, but it cannot necessarily be assumed that all local governments constitute the 'periphery' of a society and central government the 'centre' such that we can transpose the study of centre–periphery relations into central–local relations of an intergovernmental nature. If we did problems would arise in studying highly centralized states where local governments do not exist, because we would be led into believing that these states did not have 'peripheries'. This point is made clearer in introducing the second qualification. The politico-spatial dimension is evidently 'spatial' in nature but is not necessarily determined by space or distance. If it were, centre–periphery relations would be reduced to questions of geometry or geography. As Edward Shils (1961: 117) has noted:

> The central zone is not, *as such*, a spatially located phenomenon. It almost always has a more or less definite location within the bounded territory in which the society lives. Its centrality has, however, nothing to do with geometry and little to do with geography.

What, then, does its centrality have to do with? Shils argues that the centre of a society is defined in terms of the dominant value system of the society and thus in terms of the presence of authority and consensus. The centre, then, is that location which embodies the value system by which a society is ordered and by which authority and legitimacy is accorded to the regime. It follows that the periphery is defined in terms of those parts of society where the dominant values do *not* exist:

> As we move from the centre of society, the centre in which authority is possessed, to the hinterland or the periphery over which authority is exercised, attachment to the value system becomes attenuated. (119)

Evidently, geographical factors (or distance in spatial terms) might have a role in determining the spatial location of the centre (or 'centres') and periphery (or 'peripheries') but it is more likely that nonspatial factors will have greater effect. Meny and Wright, for example, refer to the importance of 'distance in economic, cultural, social, ethnic, political, or even psychological terms, in the sense that such distance may engender the feeling of dependence towards the place or places which propagate the dominant values, ideas or norms of society' (Meny and Wright 1985: 1). This is not to deny the importance of the territorial nature of centre–periphery relations. On the contrary, the territorial dimension becomes the most important reflection of the conflictual relationship between centre and periphery simply because public authority takes on a territorial form and has a tendency to extend spatially from a given location (or locations).

The above points, however, suggest that centre–periphery relations, by definition, are not 'static', nor even simply 'fluid', but 'dynamic'. Defining centres and peripheries in terms that go beyond mere territorial location to introduce factors which underlie the value system of a society means that the conflictual nature of centre–periphery relations are best understood in the context of the development of the state and society and the forces of change and resistance to that development. We can now turn to the Italian case.

II

Centre and periphery in Italy

Centre–periphery relations in Italy have developed along two closely interrelated dimensions. First, the lateness of Italian Unification (1861) left the nascent nation-state to contend with a diverse and fragmented society because of the extent to which local and regional territorial identities had become entrenched by then. One of the main intellectual and political debates in Italy in the late nineteenth century – whether to make Italy a regional, federal or centralized state – reflected this. Italy's fragmented socioeconomic and political culture was used as an argument to support the positions of federalists and centralists alike. For the federalists (such as

Cattaneo), and regionalists (such as Minghetti) such a culture lent itself naturally to a decentralized structure and was viewed as the only means through which genuine unity in a diversified society could be achieved. For the centralists, on the other hand, it was precisely the fragmented nature of Italian society which should preclude any territorial dispersion of power within the state. Anything other than a strong unitary-centralized state would pose a threat to national unity. The force of the latter, essentially political, argument was sufficient to prevent any serious move to decentralize the new state on either a federalist or a regionalist basis. Some Italian historians (for example Ruffilli 1972: 425 and *passim*) have argued that the main effect of the forging of a centralized state was the accentuation, rather than attenuation, of local and regional identities. This development became most prominent with the beginning of 'mass politics', especially during and after the First World War. As Farneti (1985: 63 ff.) has shown, territorial differences became of primary importance in the political history of the country because of the way in which territorial identities became linked to Italy's developing subcultures, Catholic and Marxist. The most vivid example of this was the development of the so-called 'red belt', a socialist 'enclave' of three regions (Tuscany, Umbria and Emilia–Romagna) stretching across central Italy.

The above developments have been intertwined with a broader based centre–peripheral cleavage, that between a prosperous and rapidly developing North and a poor and underdeveloped South. The South of Italy (the *Mezzogiorno*) is an area south of an imaginary line running across the country just below Rome. It comprises eight regions (including the two islands Sicily and Sardinia), 43 per cent of the land area and approximately 38 per cent of the population. It is, therefore, larger than a number of West European countries. Its backwardness, which has become known as the 'Southern Question' *(Questione Meridionale)*, and which successive postwar governments have committed themselves to resolving, has been characterized by two aspects. The first is an underdeveloped economy. In the immediate postwar period the South still had most of the features of an underdeveloped economy. Income per head was less than a half of that of the North; unemployment was as high as 50 per cent in some areas; industry was virtually nonexistent and consisted largely of artisan and small workshops. The second aspect refers to culture and values. Southern culture has generally been regarded as primitive in the form of the persistence of illiteracy (in 1951, for example, one in four Southerners were illiterate) and the maintenance of individualistic, as opposed to group, values. Its difference to the cultural norms of the North is symbolized in the influence of the Mafia and clientelistic practices. In its early form the Mafia was a welcome presence in the South because it carried out a role normally reserved to the state: the maintenance of authority. The problems of the South persist to this day. Indeed, even though living standards have improved there in the postwar period, they have improved three times as fast in the North, thus increasing the gap between North and South.[1]

In short, the development of the centre and periphery in Italy confirms the potential complexity of this dimension as indicated earlier. The dimension has emerged not only in the form of a fragmented society with centrifugal trends and consequent 'strong' peripheries but also in the form of territorial dualism, with a large peripheral area in the South. Moreover, the two dimensions have developed in intimate relation to each other. A consistent theme, for example, in the calls for a further strengthening of the periphery (through the creation of autonomous subnational governments) has been the 'self-development' of the South (see Mori 1981 for a recent survey).

What is the exact nature of the conflictual relationship between centre and periphery in Italy, particularly in the context of the development of Italian politics and society? Answering this question depends to a large degree on what one considers the essential paradigms of development in a nation-state to be. Three such paradigms are usually recognized (see for example Tarrow 1977; Cox, Furlong and Page 1985). They will be outlined and their applicability to the Italian case evaluated.

III

Value 'spread': the periphery's ability to resist

For authors such as Shils (1961), the development of society is a process by which the centre's values are extended to the periphery. The periphery, in this view, is not just the places where these values have not penetrated but the places which, for whatever reason, have resisted the diffusion of the centre's values. The fundamental conflicts in society, therefore, relate to those between the groups and institutions which seek to diffuse the centre's values (society's elites), and those that resist them.

Explaining the conflictual nature of centre–periphery relations in terms of a conflict over values finds obvious application to Italy with its North–South cleavage. The South, in fact, has been an important area for the fieldwork of anthropologists, sociologists and behaviourists seeking to explain why it has failed to escape abject poverty and backwardness. Edward Banfield (1958 and 1971), for example, studied a small village in the South of Italy (Montegrano, a pseudonym) and concluded that the explanation for backwardness was to be found in the peasants' own value-system, which he defines as 'amoral familism'. 'Amoral familism', he writes, 'is not a normal state of culture.' It is a state of culture with Hobbesian characteristics since amoral familists act according to one rule: 'Maximise the material, short-run advantage of the nuclear family; assume that all others will do likewise.' This explains, for Banfield, 'the political incapacity' of Montegrano, that is 'the inability of the villagers to act together for their common good or, indeed, for any end transcending the immediate, material interest of the nuclear family'. The pursuit of these interests prevents the diffusion of the values of the centre, based as they are on consensus, trust, authority and the notion of community action. Indeed, for Banfield, only the presence of the state (in the form of the police) and the fear of reprisals from injured parties prevent the outbreak of a Hobbesian 'war of all against all', since the only people to whom amoral familists apply moral standards of right and wrong are members of their family.

Banfield's thesis has been modified somewhat by others who have carried out fieldwork in the south of Italy (see, for example, Cancian 1961; Silverman 1968; Galtung 1974), but these approaches all share an important feature: that while it is recognized that there may be a variety of factors which contribute to backwardness, the overriding factor is the peasant ethos or culture which can be viewed as an independent variable determining the resistance of the periphery to the diffusion of the centre's values. In Banfield's words (1958: 24):

> ...for purposes of analysis and policy the moral basis of the society may usefully be regarded as the strategic, or limiting factor. That is to say, the situation may be understood, or altered, better from this standpoint than from any other.

The weaknesses in this argument are evident and well noted (for example Pizzorno 1966; Muraskin 1974). First, it views the development of society in a unidirectional manner. The centre is clearly defined in terms of the principal cultural mores of society, while the periphery is simply defined in terms of its tendency to resist the values and norms emanating from the centre. There is no consideration of the possible effects of the centre's attempt to penetrate the periphery with its values. The possibility of initiative from the periphery, for example, of an outward diffusion of *its* values, is precluded. Banfield and others, of course, would argue that their findings refute the validity of such a criticism because of the discovery of a value-system which is fundamentally defensive and 'anticommunity' in nature. This leads, however, to a more specific weakness, which is that this type of approach denies the existence of external, 'objective' factors in determining the political behaviour of the periphery.

For Banfield, the Southern peasant's action is determined purely by his values (which may or may not have been conditioned by his environment). Yet verification of this is possible only if it can be shown that an alternative pattern of behaviour is, in fact, possible. In other words, to prove that the peasant's behaviour is determined by 'amoral familism' Banfield has to show first, that the peasant of Montegrano has the possibility of taking an alternative course of action to the one he takes of resisting the penetration of the centre; and secondly, that, if he did take that alternative course of action, it would actually have the required effect. Otherwise his analysis is simply a study of behaviour which purports to be determined by a value-system. In fact, much of Banfield's work contradicts his thesis because it tends to show, first, that the objective circumstances in which the people of Montegrano find themselves preclude the possibility of alternative action, and secondly, that even if they were able to take alternative action the conditions in Montegrano would not improve anyway. The people of Montegrano, then, are not acting on the basis of 'amoral familism' but on the basis of rationality: they are aware that nothing in fact can be done for Montegrano through collective action (Pizzorno 1966: 59). As Muraskin (1974: 1494) notes:

> Banfield has falsely assumed that values, ideals, and needs can be discovered from how people act without reference to the external constraints that confine them.[2]

This, as Pizzorno indicates, changes the orientation of the enquiry from asking why the Montegranians do nothing to asking why can nothing be done in Montegrano. In other words, the question is not why the periphery resists values emanating from the centre – because it is not proven that it does – but why the periphery is unable to escape its status as the periphery. This changes the conflictual nature of the relationship through shifting emphasis to the centre and its power to dominate the relationship.

IV

Value 'penetration': the centre's ability to dominate

The concept of 'historical marginality' (Pizzorno 1966) counters the idea that capitalist society develops through a diffusion of values from centre to periphery, with the periphery being able to resist the spread of those values. It is accepted that the development of the capitalist market system leads to greater integration of society, but it is argued that at the same time it generates new forms of differentiation. There is an ever greater concentration of political and economic activity in certain areas, a rise in importance of functional over territorial cleavages (Shonfield 1965), greater investment in urban rather than rural areas and consequently a growing difference in the quality of life between the cities and the countryside. This form of economic marginality, which is most characteristic of the peasantry (Franklin 1969), makes it increasingly difficult for the peripheral areas to escape by integrating with the developing areas. It is not, then, that the periphery *resists* the *values* that emanate from the centre, but that it cannot, as a result of the natural imbalance inherent in capitalist development, *obtain* the *resources* necessary to overcome its subordination. Its 'integration', therefore, takes on a distorted form: it is relegated to performing residual economic activities and it provides a reservoir of labour through migration. Indeed, migration is the only alternative to waiting for capitalist development to spread territorially to these areas.

Even waiting may prove fruitless, however, for it is not necessarily always the case that the centre ignores the periphery. On the contrary, for many authors it is the intervention of the state in an attempt to industrialize the periphery that creates an economy which may be less poor but more dependent upon the centre (see for example Hechter 1975). Rather than the centre failing to penetrate the periphery, then, the marginality perspective points to the penetration of the periphery by the centre and its consequent effects. The conflictual nature of the relationship is an imbalanced one which always favours the centre. Such penetration may have a distinct political goal: the retention of the peripheral status of the periphery in order to preserve the power wielded at the centre.

The North–South divide in Italy is in many ways exemplary of these arguments, and particularly those emphasizing the political rationale behind state intervention. Writers of the Left in Italy – and particularly

Marxists – have argued that the origins of the 'Southern Question' lie in the way in which Unification was achieved in 1860. Antonio Gramsci (1926; 1971), for example, probably the most important Italian Marxist thinker and one of the founders of the Italian Communist Party (PCI), argued that Unification was achieved through an alliance between the Northern industrial bourgeoisie and the Southern landed aristocracy. The former were the main promoters of Unification and this found support amongst radical elements in the South (epitomized by the action of Garibaldi). The landed aristocracy in the South feared the consequences for its own position of Unification particularly if carried through as a revolution 'from below'. They offered, therefore, to support the North's attempt to achieve Unification and subsequent policies for the nascent nation-state on condition that the *status quo* was maintained in the South, that is that the aristocracy's control of the land, and thus domination of the peasantry, was left untouched. As a result of this alliance – or, in Gramsci's words, 'historic bloc' – governmental economic policy constantly favoured the North while leaving the South under the control of the landowners in return for their support of the regime. This form of patronage did not greatly alter under Fascism because the Fascists came to a similar agreement with the South. By 1943 (when Fascism was overthrown) the North was an industrial developing economy while the South remained a largely under-developed agricultural economy.

For Gramsci, however, the nature of the centre's penetration and domination of the periphery was not purely an economic form of power, as classical Marxism suggested. He argued that power in capitalist society is not solely based on the economic system of production and exchange. Rather, it is based on a dialectical relationship between the structure and superstructure of society, the latter being defined as philosophy, ideology, culture and so on. The combination of these two forms the basis of the ruling bloc's 'hegemony', whereby the ruled accept the ruling class's intellectual and moral values. This assigns a key role to intellectuals: the most active elements of the intelligentsia are won over to the prevailing ideology which helps maintain the domination of the economically under-developed areas. The 'Southern intellectual' (epitomized in Benedetto Croce and Giustino Fortunato) provided the essential intellectual under-pinning of the industrial agrarian bloc:

> ...the Southern citizen is linked to the big landowner through the intellectual. This is the most common type of relationship on the Southern mainland and in Sicily. It constitutes a monstrous agrarian bloc which functions overall as an

intermediary and guardian for Northern capitalism and the big banks. Its sole purpose is the conservation of the *status quo*. (Gramsci 1926: 153; author's translation)

For Gramsci, therefore, the class cleavage in Italy had expressed itself in a peculiarly territorial form. This explained the development of political movements and parties of a 'regionalist' or 'Southern' nature, which impeded the development of a system of values which could counter those of the historic bloc. Regionalism was regarded as a natural expression of the historic bloc's attempt to defuse opposition to it by dispersing the exploited class's aspirations on a territorial basis, thus blurring the essential class nature of exploitation. It can be argued that the postwar period experienced a similar turn of events. In the same way that they had switched their support to Fascism so the Southern landowners, in the post-Fascist period, switched their support to the prospective dominant political party, the Christian Democrats (DC). However, the DC, once in power, gradually removed its dependence on the Southern landowners' support in two ways: first, through land reform, which, in giving land to the peasants, removed the linchpin of the landowners' control; and second, through replacing the form of patronage based on the individual landowner with a form of patronage based on the party and state. It did this by expanding the public sector of the economy (the 'parastate') through the creation of hundreds of bureaucratic agencies and staffing these agencies with party personnel. The state bureaucracy became a vast dispenser of patronage which was used to buy support for the DC. It is in this context that state intervention in the South should be considered. An official policy for the industrialization and development of the South began in 1950. It was based on a programme of aids and incentives to private industry combined with direct intervention on the part of state industries. Yet nearly forty years later the South remains a poor and more dependent economy, relying upon massive transfers of funds from the North: an autonomous mechanism of self-sustaining industrial development has not been initiated. One of the main reasons put forward to explain this is that the policies which have been adopted have rarely been governed by the economic needs of the South, but by the economic interests of the North and the political needs of the DC. In other words, state intervention has occurred where it will garner support for the party. The party, in turn, has acted as the guardian of the interests of Northern capital.[3] The DC, in short, has been in the words of one commentator 'the Gramscian party in reverse' (Halliday 1968: 92).

An approach which stresses the penetration and domination of the periphery by the centre qualifies the view of the periphery as a resistant force to change. It nonetheless rests on the same assumption as the approaches which view the periphery in this way in that it precludes any initiative on the part of the periphery (Banfield's first weakness noted earlier). In other words, the periphery may want to escape its role as the periphery but it cannot do so by its own means. It is dependent on the workings of the capitalist system, and this system may even be operated to ensure that the periphery fails to escape its peripheral status. This overlooks the possibility that the effects of the market and state intervention may not be watertight. In addition, Marxist analyses assume that class cleavages, while possibly taking on a territorial form, will nonetheless cut across territorial cleavages. The South of Italy remains the periphery apparently because it is in the interests of the bourgeoisie of that area to keep it that way. Sidney Tarrow (1977) has raised the question, however, of whether the local bourgeoisie can always be regarded as simply a link in the chain of capitalistic domination by the centre. Is it not possible that, under certain circumstances, the local bourgeoisie will act to improve the position of the periphery? If so, how can local elites act on behalf of the periphery? This introduces the intergovernmental dimension of centre-periphery relations and the possibility of a diffusion of the periphery's values outwards.

V

Value 'interchange': the periphery as an active agent

That there is space for initiative on the part of the periphery has been shown through the work of authors such as Sidney Tarrow (1977) and others (see Graziano, Katzenstein and Tarrow 1978). They argue that the distribution of power between the centre and periphery can be properly evaluated only through reference to the institutional structures – parliaments, the bureaucracy and political parties – which link the centre and the periphery. The operation of these allows the periphery to develop marginal political power to compensate for its economic marginality. In Tarrow's words (1977: 26):

> The periphery can plausibly compensate for its economic marginality by seeking the intercession of the state on its behalf.

There are two reasons for this. The first is that the process of concentration of political and economic power at the summit of the political system and the increasing importance of functional over territorial cleavages can, Tarrow argues, generate precisely the opposite effect on citizens' perception of the importance of the territorial dimension of power. In other words, those at the periphery, seeing the location and exercise of power become increasingly remote, are likely to turn to their local territorial representatives to protect their interests. As a result, sensitive policy areas have had a tendency

> to unite groups within localities against the centre and challenge the hegemony of the functional interest groups that tended to overawe localities in the 1950s and early 1960s. (Tarrow *et al.* 1978: 22)

The second reason why peripheral initiative is a possibility is that the state cannot be regarded as a singular, rational, efficient entity. To argue this, Tarrow draws on organizational theory and particularly that associated with Michael Crozier (1966; 1973). Crozier's study of state bureaucracies shows that while bureaucracies first emerged to rationalize the functioning of society their internal dynamics frequently lead to new forms of inefficiency, with the actual operation of the organization becoming increasingly divorced from the way in which it should function. Tarrow applies this theory to the institutional structures existing between centre and periphery. He argues that the degree of dysfunctionalism that exists means that the same organizational structures that allow the centre to regulate the periphery also provide a channel for the periphery to influence the centre. To confirm this his analysis shows how local elites in Italy and France adopt different strategies to garner resources from the centre, according to prevailing national conditions. In France, which is characterized by a hierarchical and efficient administrative system, the local leader becomes an 'administrative activist', seeking through his ties with the bureaucracy to capture the benefits his community needs. In Italy, on the other hand, the local leader is confronted with a bureaucracy which is fragmented, inefficient and prone to clientelistic practices. As a result he becomes a 'political entrepreneur' in which he seeks benefits for his community not only through the bureaucracy but through the party system and personal contacts in the capital.[4]

In this view of centre–periphery relations local elites become essentially gatekeepers of the periphery, who, using their skills as political actors, attempt to promote change at the periphery. Such aspects as patronage, then, cannot be viewed simply as instruments of the centre to dominate the periphery because they can be exploited by local elites to further the ends of their own communities. Indeed, Tarrow (1977: 248) argues that although the French mayor gains more than his Italian counterpart from a more efficient system, to do so he must nonetheless 'accept the technocratic values of the policy elite'. The Italian mayor, on the other hand, while gaining less from a clientelistic system, has a greater chance 'to use the resources he gains for goals that correspond to the policy values of his party'.

Criticisms of this approach have focused on the degree of peripheral leverage possible, and how widespread such leverage is likely to be. On the assumption that the local elites will indeed act on behalf of the periphery rather than the central elites (with whom they may share the same political party), divisions within the periphery might still inhibit or damage their attempts to garner resources from the centre. Cox, Furlong and Page (1985: 171–2), for example, argue that the limitations on peripheral leverage are severe, and one might wonder how much leverage, for example, the mayor of Montegrano can wield.

This approach has nonetheless considerable validity in the Italian case if viewed from the perspective of the development and integration of society. Rather than value 'spread' or value 'penetration' it suggests that the process of value integration in society can be 'two way'. Whatever the precise role of the centre in the diffusion or use of its values, the very interaction between centre and periphery provides a diffusion in the reverse direction as well. As Graziano (1978: 291) has argued, the significant point about Italy's development is that it is not clear which of the 'two nations', North and South, has had the greater impact in terms of values. Indeed, of note is the extent to which the South has been able to condition the entire course of Italian development through its influence over the state. Most analyses of the Italian state (for example Amato 1976; Di Palma 1979; Donolo 1980) stress the extent to which it is inefficient, 'fragmented' and based upon clientelistic practices. These practices, as indicated earlier, had their origins in the South and its traditional system of patronage. Rather than the state modernizing the South, then, the South has 'southernized', or 'meridionalized', the north. If this is the case, authors such as Shils, who define the centre and periphery in terms of value 'spread', might have to think twice in deciding which, between Italy's North and South, is the 'centre' and which is the 'periphery'. Pasquale Villari had a point: the barbarians are not just a defensive formation; they also have a good attack.

VI

Conclusion

This paper has stressed the importance of viewing both dimensions – intergovernmental and politico–spatial – of the centre–periphery paradigm of power in terms of national development, the integration of society and the role of values. This perspective allows a proper evaluation of the inherently confrontational nature between the centre and periphery in all societies. If there is a problem with this perspective it is that the validity of a particular approach will depend upon the particular definitions of 'centre' and 'periphery' that one chooses to adopt. As Cox, Furlong and Page (1985: 173) note, too often in centre–periphery studies 'the participants are talking past one another'. This, however, can be viewed as a truism for the study of all dimensions of power. The existence of mutually exclusive theories simply confirms the difficulties of evaluating the concept. It should not inhibit further exploration.

Notes

1. There is an enormous literature on the underdevelopment of the South. See, for example, Allen and MacLennan 1970: pt 1; Lutz 1962; Graziani 1978; and Bongiovanni 1978.
2. Banfield himself reveals explicitly the shaky foundation of his analysis with the following (remarkable) statement: 'The coincidence of facts and theory does not "prove" the theory. However, it does show that the theory will explain (in the sense of making intelligible and predictable) [*sic*] much behaviour without being contradicted by any of the facts at hand' (Banfield 1971: 78–9).
3. For examples of this type of argument see Chubb 1982; Tarrow 1967.
4. It should be stressed that Tarrow indicates that the local leaders' strategies are determined by other factors as well.

11. Who should be Entitled to Vote in Self-determination Referenda?

Harry Beran

I

This is the century of political self-determination. After the First World War Germany, Austro-Hungary, Tsarist Russia and Turkey lost their European subject nations. After the Second World War the European powers lost their overseas colonies. As a result the number of independent states has increased from a few dozen to about 160 over the last seventy years. At the same time the right of self-determination has become enshrined in the International Covenant on Civil and Political Rights of 1966, whose Article (l) reads:

> All peoples have the right of self-determination. By virtue of that right they freely determine their political status and freely pursue their economic, social and cultural development. (United Nations 1985)

At present there are two opposed trends in the world. There are attempts at greater integration among some regional groups of independent states, most obviously in Western Europe. But there are also still dozens of peoples who seek independence from their political masters. Most of the armed conflicts since the Second World War have been struggles to establish break-away states or to reverse political divisions. This includes some of the most serious wars of the past forty years: those in Korea, Vietnam, Nigeria and Bangladesh.

These wars and separatist struggles starkly raise the theoretical questions: what are the proper normative criteria for determining political boundaries and which groups have the moral right to political independence? The International Covenant on Civil and Political Rights does not help in answering these questions since it offers no useful guidance as to what counts as a 'people' in the Article which asserts that 'All peoples have the right of self-determination'. The United Nations, in practice, acknowledges the right of self-determination only in the case of independent states and some of the colonies of the European powers.[1]

Contemporary political theorists have given little attention to these issues. This is surprising since the legitimate unity of the state is clearly a fundamental issue of political theory, and since the emergence of many other recent social and political issues has been followed promptly by a large philosophical literature. Civil disobedience, abortion, reverse discrimination and the abuse of animals in research and food production are some of the most obvious examples. One reason for this neglect may be that quite a few of the political theorists who have considered the problems mentioned above have concluded that they are not capable of theoretical solution, at least within a liberal democratic framework (Jennings 1956: 56; Dahl 1970: 59; French and Gutman 1974; Whelan 1983). Not only has this meant that these writers have not offered normative theories of political self-determination or of legitimate political boundaries, but their judgements may also have discouraged others from trying to formulate such theories.

In three previous articles I have begun an attempt to show that a normative theory of political self-determination, secession and legitimate boundaries is possible within a liberal democratic framework (Beran 1984, 1988a, 1988b; for other important discussions of this and closely related issues see Forbes 1970, Walzer 1973: 87–94, Barry 1983 and Birch 1984). The guiding principle of this theory is that the rightful unity of the liberal democratic state must be based on the consent of its members. This article takes the development of the theory a step further by considering who should be entitled to vote in self-determination referenda.

II

A liberal democratic theory of political self-determination[2]

A group which has the moral right of political self-determination has the right freely to determine its political status. Self-determination is the right of every group which:

1. has awareness of itself as a distinct group;
2. is territorially concentrated;
3. is viable as an independent political community.

This highly permissive doctrine follows from the importance liberal democratic theory must place on liberty and the individualist interpretation of popular sovereignty required by this theory.

A group has a number of options in exercising its right of self-determination; the exercise of some of them requires a willing partner. If it is not independent, it can remain part of its existing state, change its status within it, seek independence from it or merge with another state. If it is independent already, it can remain so or merge with another state. A group does not lose the right of self-determination by exercising it, for example by choosing to remain part of an existing state on a given occasion. The right, like most rights, can be overridden by other moral considerations, and circumstances can make its exercise impossible.

The liberal democratic theory of self-determination is applied to reality by the reiterated use of the majority principle. If there is a separatist group within a state, this group may specify a territory in which a separatist referendum is to be held. Assume such a referendum is held in, say, North Wysteria and that there is a majority in favour of independence from Wysteria. But since the majority in favour of secession may not be evenly distributed throughout North Wysteria, there may be an area of North Wysteria in which there is a majority against secession. Therefore, before North Wysteria's secession becomes effective, any area of North Wysteria which wishes to do so must in turn be permitted to vote whether it wishes to secede from North Wysteria and become independent on its own, or stay with the remainder of Wysteria. This reiterated use of the majority principle over any territory specified by a separatist group must yield a determinate and consistent result in the end.

In each case only the people of the territory specified by the separatists should be entitled to vote in the referendum. For, if the North Wysterians want independence but all Wysterians are allowed to vote in the referendum intended to decide the issue, then the North Wysterians could be outvoted by their fellow citizens and the unity of Wysteria would then no longer be voluntary.

This voluntarist approach to the rightful unity of the state has to be qualified in two ways. First, only groups which are viable as independent political communities have a right of self-determination. Therefore, only such groups can rightfully demand independence by virtue of this right. Still, if the unity of the state is to be based on consent, then smaller groups must, normally, also be allowed to secede if they have the opportunity to transfer to another state. Second, secession may be subject to a number of moral or practical conditions. For example, the separatist group may have to guarantee not to oppress subgroups within itself nor to prevent the rightful secession of such subgroups. Also, if the territory of the separatists includes a disproportionately high share of the economic resources of the existing state, it may have to compensate the parent state for its loss. And if the territory of the separatist state includes an area which is culturally or strategically essential to the existing state, it may have to agree to joint sovereignty over this area or to entering an appropriate bilateral treaty regarding it.

These qualifications to the right of self-determination apply if a separatist group is treated justly by the state to which it belongs. However, if the separatists were incorporated in the existing state without their consent or if they are oppressed or exploited by it, then some of the qualifications mentioned may not apply or apply only to a limited extent. A group which can escape oppression by secession, perhaps with the help of a powerful friend, must be permitted to secede first and then to offer its former oppressor whatever justice requires .

Liberal democratic theory is committed to the claim that the unity of the rightful state must be voluntary. This voluntary unity is maximized by permitting groups which wish to secede or to transfer to another state to do so, subject to the conditions stated. Within democratic theory the procedure for determining whether there is a territorially concentrated group which wishes to secede has to be the majority principle, used more than once if necessary. But majorities can exercise their right of self-determination wisely or foolishly. Hence, in addition to the procedural criterion (the majority principle) there must also be substantive criteria for determining whether to exercise the right of self-determination and if so in which way. These substantive criteria include those for determining the optimum, as distinct from minimally viable, size of political entities. R. A. Dahl (1970: ch. 2) has shown that these latter criteria point to the need for a number of levels of political organization, ranging from local community government, via intermediate organizations, to worldwide political institutions. Current world trends, already mentioned, are likely to result in an increase in the number of so-called sovereign nation-states, as some of the existing separatist movements achieve their aims; but they also point to the likelihood that these states will lose some of their sovereign powers to international political institutions. Hence, to some extent the world is moving in the direction it should according to Dahl's multi-level model of political organization.

The principle of voluntary political association can be applied at each level of government. Recent events in the Soviet Union show that secession can be a vital political issue not only at the sovereign state level (there are increasingly popular separatist movements in the Baltic soviet socialist republics) but also at the provincial level (most of the residents of the Nagarno-Karabakh region, who are Armenian, are demanding its transfer from the Azerbaijan S S Republic to the Armenian S S Republic).

As already noted a group may exercise its right of self-determination to establish a state which is smaller than the optimum size. A democrat has to believe that experience is likely to lead people to choose political entities which meet their needs. No doubt there is some evidence against this belief, but there is also some for it. The British colonies of Western Australia and Newfoundland initially declined to be part of the newly created Australian and Canadian federations, but subsequently changed their minds.

III

Who should be entitled to vote in self-determination referenda?

The theory of self-determination presented leaves many questions un-answered. Amongst the most pressing are these:

1. How small a group can have the right of self-determination and of setting up an independent state?
2. If most of the natural resources of a state are in the area that wishes to secede, what distribution of the benefits of the exploitation of these resources is required by justice after secession?
3. Who should be entitled to vote in separatist referenda?

In the third part of this paper I shall attempt to answer the last question. This attempt raises issues of greater significance than may be apparent at first.

The Kanaks (the Melanesian traditional inhabitants of New Caledonia) wish to regain political independence. For the last few years it has been French policy that the issue should be settled by referendum among the residents of New Caledonia. But because the population of about 150,000 consists of 43 per cent Kanaks, most of whom favour independence, and 57 per cent French and other immigrants, most of whom are against it, the outcome of the referendum can be determined in advance by the franchise criterion chosen. In the1987 independence referendum adults with three years' residence in New Caledonia were eligible to vote and, predictably, there was a majority in favour of continuing unity with France.[3] Some

Kanaks have demanded that only residents with at least one locally born parent should be eligible to vote; this would ensure a majority for independence as it would exclude most non-Kanaks from the vote. In 1988 the Kanaks and the French Government, in the Matignon Accord, agreed that another independence referendum will be held in 1998. On this occasion only those on the New Caledonian electoral roles in 1988 and their children will be eligible to vote. Perhaps the agreement was possible because both the Kanaks and the non-Kanaks believe that this franchise criterion gives them a chance for a majority in the referendum.

Eligibility to vote in a separatist referendum is likely to be contested in many cases where the people who seek independence are under colonial or semi-colonial domination. For wherever people of one culture dominate those of another, the former take up residence in the territory of the latter in smaller or greater numbers in order to strengthen their hold on the territory, to limit the opportunity of the dominated people for self-determination or even to assimilate them altogether. The Russians are sufficiently well known for this practice to permit us to speak of the Russification of Estonia, Latvia and Lithuania, for example. It would be equally appropriate to speak of the Sinofication of Tibet and the Indonesation of West New Guinea.

Are there any relevant, non-arbitrary criteria for determining who should be entitled to vote in a self-determination plebiscite such as that planned for New Caledonia? The criterion normally used is some period of residence in the territory in question (Farley 1986: 92–3). After the First World War a considerable number of plebiscites were held in Europe to determine political borders. The habitual resident date chosen ranged from six years prior to the plebiscite in one instance to twenty years in another (Farley 1986: 93). Because a dominant power can move people into an area and expel others from it, the habitual resident date chosen can largely determine the outcome of the plebiscite. But it is difficult to see how one period of residence rather than another can by itself be anything other than an arbitrary criterion for the franchise.

Birth in a territory (or birth in a territory where the parents are habitual residents) is another possible criterion. This could be offered as a non-arbitrary criterion. Human beings need territory to make a life for themselves. Therefore, they must have the right to live somewhere. And where better, normally, than the place where they were born and have grown into adult members of a community. Usually, they will feel that they belong there.

However, the Kanak suggestion, reported earlier, was not that only those born in New Caledonia should be enfranchised, but that only those with at least one locally born parent should be. This is obviously intended to exclude the great majority of the non-Kanaks from the independence referendum. Moreover, some of the Kanaks claim that non-Kanaks do not belong in New Caledonia, even if they feel they do.

This suggests a third criterion which flows directly from the right of political self-determination. If a group has this right it must also have the right to control immigration into its territory.[4] Otherwise a large number of immigrants could undermine the group's ability to 'freely determine their political status and freely pursue their economic, social and cultural development'. For the same reason, in a world in which 'all peoples have the right of self-determination' there cannot be a right of conquest. It follows that if a group that has the right of self-determination is conquered and the conqueror permits immigration against the wishes of the vanquished, the immigrants are there in violation of the rights of the conquered. The immigrants are there without the right of being there and, in this sense, do not belong even if they have spent their whole lives there and feel they belong. If circumstances after the conquest change so as to give the conquered people the opportunity to determine by plebiscite whether they wish to regain their independence, it seems only fair that those present among them without their consent should be enfranchised only at their discretion. For if the immigrants are numerous enough, they could, by their votes, prevent the conquered people from exercising their right of self-determination. Thus the third criterion of entitlement to vote in a self-determination plebiscite is being in a territory by moral right. This right is acquired not simply by birth in a territory, let alone by some period of residence there, but by being a member of a group which traditionally occupies a territory or by being in a territory by permission of the traditional occupants. In other words, there is a presumption that all citizens who habitually live in a territory are enfranchised to vote in self-determination plebiscites. But this presumption fails for residents living in the territory without the consent of the people who occupy the territory by right.

The third criterion seems to be the only one of those considered which is consistent with the right of political self-determination and will therefore be adopted here.

However, the use of this criterion gives rise to further problems of political theory and practice. Assume (1) that France lets the Kanaks determine who is to be enfranchised for the 1998 independence referendum (a heroic assumption indeed), (2) that the Kanaks restrict the franchise to those who have at least one locally born parent and that there is, therefore, a majority for independence, (3) that independence is achieved, but (4) that most residents are against independence and against a New Caledonian government dominated by Kanaks. If independence is achieved under these conditions and with fully democratic political institutions, then Kanak self-determination will be undermined despite independence, because the Kanaks will be dominated by their culturally very different fellow citizens who make up almost 60 per cent of the population.

If the Kanaks wish to exercise their right not to be dominated by others, there are a number of ways of avoiding this:

1. partition of the country into Kanak occupied and immigrant-occupied parts;
2. weighting of the political system in favour of the Kanaks to ensure their political dominance;
3. encouragement of voluntary emigration of non-Kanaks;
4. assimilation of non-Kanaks into the Kanak population;
5. repatriation of non-Kanaks with the cooperation of France;
6. expulsion of most non-Kanaks.

Partition of the country is intolerable to the Kanaks because of the intimate relationship of particular groups of Kanaks with particular areas of land traditionally occupied by them. It would separate a substantial proportion of Kanaks from the land from which 'the very meaning of their existence' (Dornoy 1984: 120) is derived. Weighting the political system sufficiently in favour of the Kanaks to create a Kanak-dominated government is likely to increase racial tension to the point of open conflict, perhaps even civil war. 'Voluntary' emigration of non-Kanaks in large numbers is likely only if they are oppressed or discriminated against. Assimilation of European New Caledonians into the Kanak population is impossible in practice and if forced assimilation were possible it would not be morally acceptable. French-assisted repatriation of sufficient numbers of non-Kanaks to make the Kanaks the overwhelming majority in New Caledonia is an entirely realistic policy and indeed the policy France should adopt if the Kanaks desire it.

If the Kanaks wish to exercise their right not to be dominated by immigrants present in New Caledonia against the Kanaks' wishes and if France does not agree to cooperate in a repatriation programme, would the final option – expulsion of most immigrants – be morally tolerable?

Clearly expulsion would be an evil, but perhaps it would be the least evil option available to the Kanaks.

The expulsion of immigrants for the sake of the self-determination of a conquered people may well be the least evil, morally speaking, if the following conditions hold:

1. Emperia (E) and Colonia (C) are distinct territories, with their distinct inhabitants, the Es and the Cs;
2. E has in the past annexed C by conquest;
3. C has regained independence or is attempting to regain it;
4. during the colonial period, many Es moved into C without the consent of the Cs;
5. the presence of large numbers of Es in C undermines the possibility of self-determination for the Cs;
6. the Es in C are citizens of E and, therefore, entitled to residence in E;
7. E has some moral responsibility for the presence of the Es in C and should, therefore, assist in their return to E;
8. the number of Es involved can readily be absorbed in E.

The argument for the moral permissibility of expulsion of the Es is implicit in the conditions just stated and is an extension of the previous argument for the claim that people who live in a territory in violation of the rights of the traditional occupants may legitimately be excluded from separatist referenda. A group with the right of self-determination must have the right to control immigration into its territory. Otherwise, large-scale immigration combined with fully democratic politics could make the group a minority in its own country, unable to govern itself or to control its own development. If the right to control immigration is violated, especially if it is violated to the point where the group's opportunity for self-determination is threatened, if it is readily possible for the immigrants to return to their places of origin, and if the immigrants do not depart voluntarily, then their expulsion may be morally permissible.

Perhaps some of the eight conditions listed are morally redundant. For example, it could be claimed that condition (5) is redundant since, if a group has the right of self-determination, it may expel anyone present in its territory without its consent, whether they threaten the group's opportunity for self-determination or not. After all it is a universally accepted legal principle that illegal immigrants may be expelled. But because of the gravity of expelling large numbers of people, many of whom may not be personally responsible for the predicament of the colonized group, I wish to make the case for the moral permissibility of expulsion as strong as possible. And whereas condition (4) relates to the past violation of the Cs' right of self-determination, condition (5) relates to its present violation.

New Caledonia appears to satisfy the conditions listed.[5] 1. France and New Caledonia are distinct territories. 2. France took possession of New Caledonia in 1853 when the local population was about 60,000. France not only declared sovereignty over New Caledonia but also denied that the Melanesian inhabitants had property rights in their land.

> In less than two years from the possession of New Caledonia by the French .... the local chiefly system was destroyed, and the Melanesians were dispossessed of nine-tenths of their best land and pushed into the rugged, mountainous interior.
>
> Assuming that the Melanesians would soon disappear, ... (they) were regrouped arbitrarily and stationed on limited reserves which .... were infringed upon little by little, or were situated in infertile zones not favoured by the *colons*. (Dornoy 1984: 19)

The Melanesians resisted expropriation as far as they could. Twenty-nine Melanesian attacks on Europeans occurred between 1856 and 1878. Two major revolts occurred in 1878 and 1917 but were put down by the French. In the first two hundred Europeans and over a thousand Melanesians were killed, in the second eleven Europeans and two hundred Melanesians. Dornoy suggests that the basic cause of the first uprising was 'the antagonism existing between the conquered and the conquerors' (1984: 29) and that the second uprising showed that 'the Melanesians, although conquered, were not entirely subdued' (1984: 30).

3–5. The present population of New Caledonia is approximately 150,000. It consists of about 65,000 Kanaks, mostly favouring independence, 55,000 Europeans, mostly favouring continuing union with France, and 30,000 immigrants from Micronesia, Polynesia, Indonesia, Vietnam and other areas, mostly favouring union with France as they fear repatriation under a Kanak-controlled government. The non-Kanak population has grown from a mere 15,000 in 1936 to the present 85,000 due to a vigorous immigration policy pursued by France (Dornoy 1984: 2). The Melanesian population of about 60,000 at colonization dropped to about 29,000 by 1936 due to colonial repression, introduced diseases and social evils (especially alcoholism). But since then it has recovered to its 1853 level.

At present I have no direct evidence as to whether the large-scale immigration into New Caledonia during the last fifty years, which has made the Kanaks a minority in their own country, occurred against their wishes. But it is clear that in the nineteenth and early twentieth century they vigorously resisted colonization and that, once their resistance was broken, they had little opportunity to oppose the policies of their colonial rulers. Before 1946 the Kanaks were excluded from political life. Since then they have increasingly been legally entitled to take part in politics and have become politically active. From 1969 onwards they created their own political parties and from 1975 onwards the Kanaks have favoured independence in increasing numbers. The French government 'favoured a policy of massive immigration during the boom years of the nickel industry' (1969–1970) in order to 'reinforce the French presence in New Caledonia' (Dornoy 1984: 4). In the face of Kanak resurgence it also adopted a policy of multi-racialism according to which all New Caledonians are French citizens with equal rights and duties. The Kanaks, though the original occupants of the islands, are considered to be merely one ethnic group among others (Dornoy 1984: 4). In the absence of clear evidence as to whether the Kanaks have opposed the large-scale immigration of recent decades, it seems reasonable to assume that they would have opposed being made a minority in their own country, had they had the opportunity to do so.

As previously noted, self-determination for the Kanaks, while they are a minority in New Caledonia, is not possible.

6–8. Almost all the non-Kanak inhabitants of New Caledonia are French citizens (Dornoy 1984: 50, 63–81) and are entitled to residence in metropolitan France. Recent French governments have encouraged immigration into New Caledonia and are, therefore, responsible for it. Metropolitan France could readily absorb whatever number of non-Kanaks an independent Kanak government might wish to expel.

It therefore seems reasonable to conclude that if the Kanaks wish to exercise their right of self-determination by opting for independence and Kanak self-government, and the number of non-Kanaks cannot be reduced sufficiently by voluntary emigration and French-assisted repatriation to make this possible, then the expulsion of a significant proportion of non-Kanaks may be morally permissible.

If this seems a shocking conclusion, it should be compared to that reached by John Plamenatz, not a writer known for making extremist pronouncements, in *On Alien Rule and Self-Government*. He writes there that one of the duties of a colonial power about to grant independence to a colony is to help the colonial settlers to reach a settlement with the natives which will enable them to live in harmony together after independence has come, or else, if that cannot be done, to help them withdraw from the colony with as little loss as possible. The natives are usually the great majority, and their interests must be preferred to all others, even (should the need arise) to the extent of removing from among them the alien settlers who came uninvited and often took the best of whatever was to be had. This is not required by principles generally accepted two or three hundred years ago, but it is required by principles which the West Europeans have come to adopt in recent times and which they have propagated all over the world. (1960: 99)

As already noted, the expulsion of large numbers of people from a territory where they have lived a considerable part of their lives or perhaps all of it is a great evil. It is morally acceptable only as a last resort and as a least evil. Moreover, nothing written in this paper is intended to provide any moral weight to the forced assimilation or expulsion of culturally different minorities that are no threat to the self-determination of the majority among whom they live. Justice requires that they be given minority rights to maintain and develop their own culture.

Also, as already noted, the possibility that fewer than all eight conditions may be sufficient to make expulsion permissible is left open, but any such case would require further argument.

If a number of conditions (5) to (8) are not met, expulsion is usually impermissible. Northern Ireland illustrates this. A reminder of the issues at stake may be helpful before the applicability of conditions (1) to (8) to Northern Ireland is examined. According to the liberal democratic theory of self-determination, the Nationalist Irish were entirely within their rights in demanding independence from Britain. But, on the face of it, so are the Protestants of Northern Ireland in insisting on remaining within the United Kingdom. Perhaps *only* on the face of it, since the Protestants are the descendants of the English and Scottish people planted on Irish soil by Britain in the seventeenth century, to the detriment of the Irish inhabitants of the area. If their ancestors were planted there against the wishes of the Irish and if they have not been accepted as legitimate inhabitants of the area, then according to the franchise criterion for self-determination referenda accepted above, their right to participate in such a referendum is at the discretion of the people amongst whom they were planted. But if they were indeed denied a vote and Northern Ireland became part of the Irish Republic, this would only postpone the boundary problem. For if the Protestants are given full democratic rights after the incorporation of

Northern Ireland into the Republic, they could some years later demand a separatist referendum and vote for secession from the Republic and independence in their own right or reunification with Britain. This could be prevented only by denying the Protestant descendants of the Planters the right to take part in separatist referenda for as long as they do not wish to be part of the Irish Republic, by banning separatist referenda altogether or by removing the descendants of the Planters from Ireland.

While Northern Ireland meets conditions (1) to (4) and (6), it does not meet conditions (5), (7) and (8). The present theory of self-determination, therefore, does not make the expulsion of the descendants of the people planted in Northern Ireland morally permissible.

Conditions (1) to (4) appear to apply to Northern Ireland straightforwardly. In the seventeenth century Britain expropriated almost all Irish landowners in Ulster Province, planted substantial numbers of English and Scottish settlers in Ulster and, especially after unsuccessful Irish uprisings against the Planters, severely oppressed the Irish by means of the highly discriminatory Penal Laws (Magee 1974: pt 1; Darby 1983). It is the Protestant descendants of the English and Scottish Planters who are keeping Northern Ireland out of the Irish Republic and within the United Kingdom. As British citizens the inhabitants of Northern Ireland can move to Britain without legal barriers. Condition (6), therefore, applies to Northern Ireland. However, the applicability of this condition is not important since the Irish Republic and the United Kingdom are both members of the European Community and the citizens of all member states of the Community have legal freedom of movement within it.

Conditions (5), (7) and (8) do not apply to Northern Ireland. Most importantly, condition (5) does not apply. Because the Protestant Irish who favour continuing unity with Britain are concentrated into one sixth of the area of Ireland, divided from Britain only by the North Channel, it is possible for this area to remain British without undermining the exercise of the right of self-determination by the Nationalist Irish in the far greater part of Ireland. Condition (7) does not apply, since one can hardly hold the present British people or contemporary British governments responsible for the policies of the British monarchy of the seventeenth century. Condition (8) does not apply since up to one million people would have to be expelled from Northern Ireland to resolve the self-determination issue thereby expelling the descendants of the Planters. While it would not be impossible to resettle so many people in Britain (quite a few would no doubt be accepted by the United States and other English-speaking countries), it would be extremely difficult. This would be especially so if the case for the expulsion of very large numbers of people also applied to other former British colonies. Moreover such resettlement would involve very considerable hardship for many of the people involved.

In view of these considerations, the expulsion of the descendants of the people planted in Ireland by Britain cannot be justified by the present theory of self-determination. But neither can their incorporation into the Irish Republic by force. Therefore, the legitimate union between the Irish Republic and Northern Ireland can be achieved only with the consent of the people of Northern Ireland. But it does of course follow from the theory of self-determination offered here that at least some of the areas of Northern Ireland with Catholic majorities are entitled to secede from Britain in order to join the Republic.

The present theory of self-determination does not justify a claim to sovereignty by the Irish Republic over the whole of Ireland. Perhaps there are some other arguments which justify such a claim, but their consideration is beyond the scope of this paper.

Finally, it must be mentioned that there are of course people who have been conquered and whose lands have been overrun by invaders and immigrants to such an extent that it is not now possible to remove the newcomers in order that the conquered people may have an opportunity for self-determination in all of the territories they once occupied. (Indeed some of the conquered people no longer exist.) Even if it is physically possible to return three million non-Maori New Zealanders and sixteen million non-Aboriginal Australians to their countries of origin or those of their ancestors as far as this can be determined, the political will to do so cannot be created. Moreover, the forced transfer of people on such a scale would be a greater evil than that which it would be intended to remedy. In the case of North America, it is of course literally impossible to remove the people who have occupied, nearly always unjustly, the lands of the American Indians.

In all such cases, where a full opportunity for self-determination is not possible, justice requires the adoption of the next best measures, especially those desired by the people whose opportunity for self-determination has been unjustly diminished or destroyed. These measures include political independence on the part of the territory once occupied by a people, local autonomy or special land rights for a partial exercise of the right of self-determination, or compensation for past losses if the descendants of the conquered still suffer the effects of this conquest.

In the case of Australia such measures must include special land rights for Aborigines, because of the intimate relationship between relatively small groups of Aborigines and particular areas of land located throughout Australia and because of the high priority Aborigines place on land rights.[6]

Notes

1. James Crawford (1988) explores the contrast between the universalistic language of international law and the selective practice of the United Nations regarding self-determination and the related conflict in international law between the right of all peoples to self-determination and the right of all states to territorial integrity.
2. This section presents a slightly modified summary of the theory as developed in the author's articles mentioned in the text.
3. The outcome was so predictable that many Kanaks boycotted the referendum.
4. This assumes that the group does not have far more territory than it needs, territory which is needed by another people whose territory is badly overpopulated. See Walzer 1983: 46–8.
5. Most of the factual information is drawn from Dornoy 1984.
6. In 1988 an earlier version of this paper was read in the Philosophy Department at Aberdeen University, the Politics and Ethics Department at University College Dublin, and the Government Department at the London School of Economics and Political Science. It has benefited from the discussions it received there. I am also grateful to Clare Harding and Robert Dunn for comments on the paper.

12. Self-determination and Sovereignty

Richard Tur

Treason doth never prosper: what's the reason?
For if it prosper, none dare call it treason.

(Harington 1615: 'Of Treason')

According to Dicey, Parliament has 'under the English Constitution, the right to make or unmake any law whatever and ... no person or body is recognised by the law of England as having a right to override or set aside the legislation of Parliament' (Dicey 1959: 39–40). Jennings writes:

> Parliament may remodel the British Constitution, prolong its own life, legislate *ex post facto,* legalise illegalities, provide for individual cases, interfere with contracts and authorise the seizure of property, give dictatorial powers to the Government, dissolve the United Kingdom or the British Commonwealth, introduce communism or socialism or individualism or fascism, entirely without legal restriction. (Jennings 1959: 147)

Although the concept of parliamentary sovereignty has obvious parallels with that of state sovereignty, the two concepts are distinct and the constitutional arrangements of any particular state need not accord legal supremacy to its legislature. Indeed, the more usual arrangement is that the legislature is subject to some degree of judicial review. Nonetheless, under the British Constitution, Parliament is sovereign and the exercise of state sovereignty such as ceding or annexing territory is not infrequently embodied in Acts of Parliament.[1]

Nowadays, when independence is conferred, it is usually the case that the relevant Act includes a section providing that no future Act of the United Kingdom Parliament shall extend or be deemed to extend to the newly independent country as part of its law.[2] The usual statutory provision is: 'No Act of the Parliament of the United Kingdom passed on or after the appointed day shall extend or be deemed to extend to [the country in question] as part of its law.'[3] There are many instances of such noncontroversial statutes granting complete independence.

However, earlier independence legislation, reflecting a stronger conception of Empire and of the sovereignty of the imperial parliament, maintained the possibility of the United Kingdom Parliament legislating for former colonies granted their 'independence' by Britain. Typical is the wording of the Statute of Westminster, 1931, Section 4 which provided that no Act was to extend or to be deemed to extend to a Dominion as part of its law unless the request and consent of that Dominion was expressly declared in the Act.

Still earlier legislation and most notably the Colonial Laws Validity Act, 1865 retained power in the Imperial Parliament to legislate for a colony even without the colony's request and consent, provided that it was made applicable 'by the express words or necessary intendment' of the Act, and by Section 2 any colonial legislation repugnant to such Imperial Act was void and inoperative.

Although absolutist conceptions of Parliamentary and of state sovereignty have been decreasingly credible in the twentieth century (see Heuston 1961; Kelsen 1966: 581–8), Parliament has on occasion wholly retained to itself power to legislate for a territory even where it has established a legislature within such a territory. Thus the Government of Ireland Act, 1920, which created a legislature and executive for Northern Ireland, did not curtail the Westminster Parliament's continuing legislative authority over Northern Ireland, and Section 75 expressly provided that the power of Parliament was undiminished in respect of Northern Ireland. The proposals for the establishment of a legislative assembly in Edinburgh which were ultimately contained in the subsequently repealed Scotland Act, 1978, likewise preserved a general legislative power for the Westminster Parliament to pass laws for Scotland.

Such ambivalence is unsurprising in that governments, no less than individuals, may well wish to keep open a range of options including contradictory options. Thus may 'independence' be granted with strings attached, not least the residual power of the Imperial Parliament to legislate directly despite the grant of legislative competence.

Again, it may be expedient to regard another 'state' as sovereign for some purposes but dependent for others. In *Duff Dev. Co. Ltd* v *The Government of Kelantan* ([1924] A C 797) the British government declared that Kelantan was a sovereign state in the Malay Peninsula in spite of the fact that there was an agreement between Great Britain and Kelantan, dated 22 October 1910, according to which Kelantan should have no relations with any foreign power except through the King of Great Britain.

The agreement also provided that 'nothing in this agreement shall affect the administrative authority now held by the Rajah of Kelantan'.

In the House of Lords, Viscount Finlay, speaking for the majority, stated:

> While there are extensive limitations upon its [Kelantan's] independence, the enclosed documents [including the agreement of 22 October 1910] do not negative the view that there is quite enough independence left to support the claim to sovereignty. But ... the question is not for us at all; it has been determined for us by His Majesty's Government, which in such matters is the appropriate authority by whose opinions the Courts of His Majesty are bound to abide. ([1924] A C 797, 816)

Notwithstanding the settled practice of the Court to take judicial notice of the status of any foreign government, and for that purpose, in any case of uncertainty, to seek information from the Secretary of State and to treat that information as conclusive, Lord Carson, dissenting, was moved to state:

> My Lords, I must confess that if it was open to me to disregard the statements contained in the letter from the Secretary of State for the Colonies, that 'Kelantan is an independent State and the present Sultan is the present sovereign ruler thereof', I would find great difficulty in coming to that conclusion of fact, having regard to the terms of the documents enclosed in the letter from the Secretary of State. It is, in my opinion, difficult to find in these documents the essential attributes of independence and sovereignty in accordance with the tests laid down by exponents of international law. ([1924] A C 797, 830)

Indeed, Counsel for the Appellants had argued that Kelantan's relationship with Great Britain was 'wholly inconsistent with the idea of an independent sovereignty as that term is understood by jurists of repute [such as Kluber, Vattel, Calvo, Wheaton and Halleck]' ([1924] A C 797, 800).

In tracing the nature of sovereignty it is, perhaps, more appropriate to consider the deliverances of current international law and legal theory rather than the self-serving and ideological claims of any particular state as to or about sovereignty. One conception which, I submit, can be disposed of readily enough is sovereignty as an absolute power to force others including other states to behave as commanded. Even the most powerful of states is unable, by force alone, to secure the obedience of all its own subjects, let alone the subjects of other states and such states themselves. Hume points out that even the most despotic and tyrannical of rulers must lead his officials (or officers) as men rather than merely compel them as animals to do his bidding.[4] Of course, with the allegiance of some, a ruler or state can compel the obedience of others, but in both domestic and international affairs such allegiances respond to and in turn influence the ever-changing balance of power.

In any event physical power, a matter of fact, can never be an adequate basis for the elucidation of 'sovereignty' which is essentially a normative concept implying authority and the legitimate use of physical power. Augustine long ago raised the question: 'Without justice, what are states but robber bands enlarged ?' (Augustine 1900: iv, 4) and although Austin taught that law is in effect the Gunman Situation writ large, the modern tendency in legal theory has been to emphasize the normative element. If, however, 'sovereignty' is supreme legal authority, it is not a mere matter of fact but a matter of interpretation and presupposition. Thus, I tend to agree with Professor Hare who holds that 'to acknowledge a government or régime as lawful is not, when this is a first-order judgment, to state any *facts* about it' (Hare 1967: 172). It is, indeed, to make a judgement of value.

Professor Hare's 'Jacobite' and his 'Scottish Nationalist' (157) may heroically hold firmly to their respective views that some Bavarian Prince is the rightful King of England and that the Act of Union, 1707, is not binding upon the Scottish people but, as we shall see, constitutional and international legal doctrine regards effectiveness as a condition of validity and would now regard Elizabeth II as the rightful Queen of England (and of Scots[5]) and the Act of Union, 1707 as unequivocally binding. In both historical and legal reality, the claims of Bavarian princes and of an invalid Act of Union may be consigned to the dustbin of lost causes and while Professor Hare's 'Jacobite' and his 'Scottish Nationalist' are not talking 'nonsense' (in the philosophically technical sense of that term) what they have to say is historically, legally and sociologically nonsensical and unreal.

Although it is usual to speak of states as 'sovereign' and to contemplate a community of many states, this way of thinking is jurisprudentially problematical in that if any state were regarded as being the supreme legal authority, then that state could not be regarded as being subject to international legal obligations. Furthermore, if 'sovereignty' is supreme legal authority, then only one and not all states could be regarded as sovereign. It follows that a state can be 'sovereign' only in the relative sense that there is no system of law, other than the international legal order, superior to the state.

It is possible, and wholly consistent with the national and international legal data, to regard any one, but only one, state as the supreme legal authority. International law would then be valid only by virtue of its having been recognized by that state and recognition of the validity of other states would follow only from the recognition of the international legal rules that determine the conditions of statehood. It follows, from such a point of view, that all law, national and international, is valid only by virtue of the presupposed validity of the national legal system from which one starts. The difficulties inherent in such statal solipsism are obvious in that no two or more states can consistently claim to be sovereign in this sense and yet, ideologically, that is precisely what many states assume and claim.

If, however, one does accept the primacy of international law then the 'sovereignty' of states is necessarily a relative sovereignty granted according to the rules of international law establishing the criteria of statehood. Not least in importance, here, is the principle of effectiveness. It is an essential function of international law to determine the conditions under which a territory and a people constitute a state at international law.

One important component in the equation is the capacity to maintain a relative degree of stability and order: 'A coercive order of human behaviour is valid law, and the community constituted by it, a State in the sense of international law, for that territory and population with regard to which the coercive order remains permanently efficacious' (Kelsen 1945: 350). This is obviously a version of the 'might is right' approach that Professor Hare criticizes. However, he admits that this approach is 'very plausible' so long as we 'leave morals out of it' and it clearly makes sense to 'say that Mr Kosygin's [or Mr Gorbachev's] regime, and not the descendants of the Tsar (if any), is the lawful government of Russia simply because its writ runs in Russia and theirs do not' (Hare 1967: 159). If, however, we do not leave morals out of it and treat the word 'lawful' as involving not merely a legal but also a moral value judgement then, clearly the 'might is right' approach precludes us from making moral judgements that we might wish to make and which a latter-day Tsarist would wish to make.

At this point an obvious conflict emerges between the criteria and deliverances of two different normative interpretations of the data. In some sense of the expression the 'might is right' approach is embedded in the legal point of view. The moralist who objects to the implications of this doctrine and who denies it any legitimacy is substituting a different system of values for those constituting the international legal order and must therefore regard international law as merely so much fact to be evaluated.

It seems to me that we can adopt either the moral or the legal point of view but not both simultaneously.

If we adhere to the (international) legal point of view of the state as (relatively) sovereign then we must acknowledge that the rules of international law, including the principle of effectiveness, apply to states. It follows that illegal acts achieving a firmly established situation (eventually) give rise to new legal rights and duties: *ex injuria ius oritur*. Within a national legal system exhibiting highly developed executive, legislative and judicial branches of government the principle *ex injuria ius oritur* can have only a very limited effect and although civil disobedience remains an option it carries with it no guarantee of success (see Tur 1985: 186). It is instructive that Professor Hare's 'Scottish Nationalist' was imprisoned (Hare 1967: 157).

However, in the relatively decentralized international legal system with actors of very different power, it is difficult to see what, short of war, can be done in the face of a powerful state flouting the law. A state sufficiently unjust to break the law is unlikely to yield up the fruits of such unlawful action other than under threat or use of effective force. Grotius observed: 'Judgments are efficacious against those who feel that they are too weak to resist; against those who are equally strong or think they are, wars are undertaken' (Grotius (1913): Proleg., sec. 25). Indeed, the historic doctrine of the 'just war' supposes that in some circumstances, as for example reaction to another state's unlawful action, war is a legitimate and justified option. It must be very clear, however, that the parties to any war will have very different views as to the justice of the matter even as both sides can call upon God in support. It follows that lawbreaking is an option open to a state in pursuit of its interests and that on occasion the incidence of legal rights and duties may be altered thereby. Thus, I suggest, international lawbreaking may be assimilated to civil disobedience, albeit civil disobedience on a large scale.

A consideration of constitutional law and doctrine leads to a like conclusion. Generally speaking, the courts will hold invalid any governmental action contrary to statute or, where applicable, to the constitution. However, where a constitution is wholly disregarded and either the existing government or a revolutionary group sets up under a new constitution of its own making, some courts have been ready to recognize the new regime as legitimate despite the apparent illegality of its origins (see Eekelaar 1973).

Most notable, perhaps, is *Madzimbamuto* v *Lardner-Burke N O and Others* (1968 (2) S A 284; [1968] 3 All E R 561) concerning the Unilateral

Declaration of Independence by Rhodesia on 11 November 1965. To be sure, the Judicial Committee of the Privy Council did not uphold the Appellate Division in Rhodesia but its decision appears to be based upon a belief (in the event mistaken) that the British government's counter-efforts would (ultimately) prevail. Nonetheless, even the Privy Council appears to have endorsed the principle of effectiveness as applicable in such circumstances. In the event, as history reveals, the 'illegal regime' prevailed and by virtue of the Southern Rhodesia Act, 1979, and Orders thereunder it was (belatedly) accorded recognition and legitimacy by the United Kingdom Parliament's retrospective ratification of the purported laws of the (so-called) 'illegal regime'.

The United Kingdom, however took a very different view of the legitimacy of the 'illegal regime' between 1965 and 1979, as is well illustrated by *Adams* v *Adams* ([1971] P 188), where the Attorney General intervened on the question of a British court recognizing as valid the effect of a decision of a court of the 'illegal regime'. On 9 April 1970, an English woman who had, on 29 December 1965, in Southern Rhodesia, married a man who was domiciled there, was granted a decree of divorce in the High Court of Rhodesia by Macaulay J., who was appointed a judge on 2 November 1968 under the ('illegal') 1965 Constitution. This woman desired to remarry in England but could not receive a marriage licence because the Registrar-General of Births, Deaths and Marriages would not recognize her Rhodesian divorce decree as a valid judgment of a lawful court. The woman petitioned the Court for a declaration that her Rhodesian divorce was valid but her petition was refused. The Court held that 'it would be a constitutional anomaly for our courts to recognize the validity of the acts of Macaulay J. as a *de facto* judge while the executive acts of those appointing him are refused recognition *de facto* by the executive here'.

The constitutional history of Ireland is also illustrative (see Calvert 1985: 6). The United Kingdom regarded the Easter Rising of 1916 and the election of the Provisional Government in 1918 as unlawful but, after years of insurrection, the Irish Free State was established by Parliament in 1922 which concurred, in 1949, in republican status. Professor Calvert remarks that a consequence of this 'neat and tidy' theory is that republican Ireland appears still to have Elizabeth II as Queen because His Majesty's Declaration of Abdication Act, 1936 did not, as a result of the Statute of Westminster, 1931, extend to Edward VIII's title to the Crown in respect of Ireland. The Irish view of the matter is understandably different. On independence, antiquated British laws ceased to have application when the

Irish Free State came into existence with the proclamation of the first Dail. Consequently, the Act of 1922 did not grant but merely recognized Irish independence. This leaves unsolved the knotty problem of Northern Ireland. Irish constitutional law treats it as part of the Irish state but the reality is different and the Northern Ireland Constitution Act, 1973, by Section 1 provides that Northern Ireland shall not cease to be part of the United Kingdom without the consent of the majority of the people of Northern Ireland voting in a border poll.

Professor Hare puts the example of a 'group of brigands' who seize power and make laws for the population. He suggests that the 'might is right' doctrine is too simple to cope adequately with the various questions about lawful government that such a situation raises (Hare 1967: 159) and it is clear from the complexities of the Irish and Rhodesian examples, among others, that a more sophisticated approach is appropriate. John Eekelaar offers for consideration 'some of the principles which may be pertinent to revolutionary situations' (Eekelaar 1973: 39). The nine listed include:

(a) The principle of effectiveness;
(b) The principle of legitimate disobedience to authority exercised for improper purposes;
(c) The principle that it is in the public interest that those in *de facto* impregnable control should be accorded legal recognition; i.e. that might, once established *ipso iure,* becomes right subject to the qualification, however, that this may not be the only relevant principle;
(d) The principle that government should be by the consent of the governed, whether voters or not;
(e) The principle of the right to self-determination.

Taken together such principles at least begin to tackle the question of the legitimacy of the legal doctrine *ex injuria ius oritur* in both the international and constitutional context. John Eekelaar seeks to support the principle of legitimate disobedience by reference to *Willcock* v *Muckle* ([1951] 2 KB 844), where the defendant had refused to produce his national registration identity card when a policeman demanded it in connection with a traffic offence. The police power derived from wartime legislation directed towards national security. A Divisional Court of seven judges upheld the absolute discharge given to the defendant and encouraged other magistrates to do likewise. This, for Eekelaar, 'amounts to an assertion that disobedience to this law is justified' and he concludes that 'the courts may take cognizance of criteria according to which unlawful acts may be justified' (Eekelaar 1973: 38).

Article 1 of the Universal Declaration of Human Rights states un-equivocally that 'All peoples have the right to self-determination'. In combination with some or all of the other principles listed above this produces the conclusion that revolutionary activity may be justified. A 'people' may, consistently with international and constitutional legal doctrine, disregard the current constitutional arrangements and repudiate the 'sovereignty' that a state may claim. In thus asserting a right to self-determination there may be sufficient justification for breaking the laws defining their existing constitutional and international status. By defini-tion any such lawbreaking is 'revolutionary' in legal terms, but it is no part of this thesis that violent revolution is necessary or desirable. Passive resistance may be a highly effective means to achieve the self-determina-tion sought. Nonetheless attempts at liberation not infrequently meet reaction and any 'people' seeking self-determination, especially by means of unlawful action, cannot discount the possibility of armed conflict.

Secession is the action of seceding or formally withdrawing from an alliance, federation or political or legal organization. Secession may be by agreement but as John Finnis observes, 'devolution of authority from the Imperial Crown in Parliament has been followed, rather regularly, by revolution within the new states of the Commonwealth' (Finnis 1973: 44). One explanation is to be found in the surprising doctrine of autochthony which requires that the authority of the new constitution spring indi-genously from the newly created state itself rather than flow derivatively from the Imperial power. Such a doctrine, founded upon the primacy of national law and upon statal solipsism, is inconsistent with the authority of the principles of international law that go to the justification of indepen-dence and secession by agreement or otherwise. Where self-determination is asserted against a recalcitrant power, in law as in life nothing succeeds like success, but a break-away state may face a long and possibly violent struggle before achieving recognition, either at international law or from the sovereign states whose laws it defied, as is illustrated by the fate of the eleven Southern states that attempted to secede from the Union in the American War of Secession of 1861 to 1865.

Article 1 of the Treaty of Union of 1707 between England and Scotland provides that 'the two Kingdoms of Scotland and England shall upon the first day of May next ensuing the date hereof and forever after be united into one Kingdom by the name of Great Britain . . .'. There have been waves of nationalist fervour over the years directed towards achieving an independent Scotland and it has been suggested that were the Scottish National Party ever to win a majority of the seats in Scotland and were the Westminster Parliament to remain unsympathetic some form of unilateral declaration would be appropriate. Clearly any such unilateral secession would be fraught with legal and practical difficulties and obviously given the unequivocal terms of the Treaty of Union any such declaration would be unlawful from the point of view of the British constitution. Nonetheless, that such a declaration would be unlawful has never been treated by Scottish Nationalists as a conclusive reason against it and secession, should certain eventualities materialize, remains an element within some strands of Nationalist thought.

By virtue of the European Communities Act, 1972, Britain is a member of the European Economic Communities and both state and Parliamentary sovereignty have been compromised thereby. In *Blackburn* v *Attorney General* ([1971] 1 WLR 1037, 1039), Lord Denning observed that 'it does appear that if this country should go into the common market and sign the Treaty of Rome, it means that we will have taken a step which is irreversible. The Sovereignty of these islands will thenceforward be limited. It will be shared with others; . . . many regulations made by the European Economic Community will become automatically binding on the people of this country'. Lord Denning perhaps overstates the case. No doubt it would be difficult for Britain now to extricate itself from Europe if, indeed, it wanted to; but it is counter-intuitive and contrary to the established doctrines of international and constitutional law to treat membership as 'irreversible'.

Professor Heuston (1961) notes that in 1913 when the Home Rule Bill was about to become law, Dicey, an ardent Unionist, in spite of all his commitment to Parliamentary sovereignty, ultimately 'jettisoned the constitution and pledged himself to armed resistance to lawful authority: he signed the Ulster Covenant'. Sir William Anson, also a devotee of Parliamentary sovereignty, did not pledge himself to civil disobedience but he observed: 'if the covenanters meet [the Home Rule Act] with armed resistance, I for one believe, with a conviction which no results of a general election can alter, that they are justified in their resistance' (cited in Heuston 1961: 200). As in international and constitutional doctrine and practice, so in the view of these great lawyers, sovereignty, be it statal or Parliamentary, may be compromised or overridden by political and moral principles and values.

Notes

1. Anglo-German Agreement Act, 1890 (Heligoland); Island of Rockall Act, 1972.
2. Kenya Independence Act, 1963, S. l; Kiribati Act, 1979, S. 1(2).
3. Mauritius Independence Act, 1968, S. 1(2); Canada Act. 1982, SS. 1 & 2.
4. 'As Force is always on the side of the governed, the governors have nothing to support them but opinion. It is, therefore, on opinion only that government is founded; and this maxim extends to the most despotic and most military governments, as well as to the most free and most popular. The soldan of Egypt, or the emperor of Rome, might drive his harmless subjects, like brute beasts, against their sentiments and inclination. But he must, at least, have led his *mamalukes* or *praetorian bands*, like men, by their opinion.' (Hume 1963: 'Of the First Principles of Government', 29).
5. See *MacCormick* v *Lord Advocate* (1953) S C 396 concerning a Scottish Nationalist challenge to the validity of the Royal Titles Act, 1953.

Bibliography

Adams, J. (1985) *The Financing of Terror,* London: New English Library

Alexander, Y. (ed.) (1976) *International Terrorism: National, Regional and Global Perspectives*, New York: Praeger

Alexander, Y. and Gleason, J. (eds.) (1980) *Behavioural and Quantitative Perspectives of Terrorism*, New York: Pergamon

Allen, K. and MacLennan, M. (1970) *Regional Problems and Policies in Italy and France*, London: Allen and Unwin

Amato, G. (1976) *Economia, Politica e Istituzioni in Italia*, Bologna: Il Mulino.

Arafat, Y. (1986) 'Today I have come bearing an olive branch and a freedom-fighter's gun', 13 November 1974, *Official Records of the General Assembly*, 29th Session Plenary Meetings, Vol 2, Verbatim Records of the 2266th to 2296th Meetings, 11 October – 22 November 1974, New York: United Nations

Aristotle (1908–52) *The Works of Aristotle translated into English*, ed. W.D. Ross, 12 vols., Oxford: Clarendon Press

Augustine (1900) *De Civitate Dei*, in J.-P. Migne (ed.) *Patrologiae Cursus Completus: Series Latina,* vol. 41, Paris: Garnier

Banfield, E. (1958) *The Moral Basis of a Backward Society*, New York: Free Press

— (1971) 'Amoral familism in southern Italy' in Dogan and Rose

Barendt, E. (1985) *Freedom of Speech,* Oxford: Clarendon Press

Barnard, E. (1971) *Wendall Wilkie: Fighter for Freedom*, Boston: Massachusetts University Press

Barry, B. (1973) *The Liberal Theory of Justice*, Oxford: Clarendon Press

— (1983) 'Self-government revisited' in Miller and Siedentop

Bassiouni, M. (ed.) (1974) *International Terrorism and Political Crimes*, Springfield, Illinois: Thomas

Bayles, M. (1970) ' The justifiability of civil disobedience', *Review of Metaphysics* 24, 1

Bedau, H. (1961) 'On civil disobedience', *Journal of Philosophy* 58, 21

— (ed.) (1969) *Civil Disobedience: Theory and Practice*, New York: Pegasus

Bell, T. (1944) *John Maclean: A Fighter for Freedom,* Glasgow: Communist Party Scottish Committee

Beran, H. (1984) 'A liberal theory of secession', *Political Studies* 32, 1

— (1987) *The Consent Theory of Political Obligation,* Beckenham: Croom Helm

— (1988a) 'More theory of secession: a response to Birch', *Political Studies*: 36, 2

— (1988b) 'Self-determination: a philosophical perspective', in Macartney

Berger, P. (1963) *An Invitation to Sociology: A Humanist Perspective,* New York: Doubleday

Berkeley, G. (1948) *Collected Works,* ed. A. Luce and T. E. Jessop, Edinburgh: Thomas Nelson

Birch, A.H. (1984) 'Another liberal theory of secession', *Political Studies* 32, 4

Bongiovanni, B. (1978) 'Questione meridionale: il diabattito nel secondo dopoguerra', in Levi, Levra and Trafaglia

Borden, M. (ed.) (1965) *The Anti-Federalist Papers,* East Lansing, Michigan: Michigan State University Press

Brown, S. (1961) 'Civil disobedience', *Journal of Philosophy* 58, 22

Buckley, Jr, W. (1970) *Did You Ever See a Dream Walking?* Indianapolis: Bobbs-Merrill

Bull, H. (1977) *The Anarchical Society,* London: Macmillan

Burton, J. (1968) *Systems States Diplomacy and Rules,* Cambridge: Cambridge University Press

Calvert, H. (1985) *An Introduction to British Constitutional Law,* London: Financial Training

Cancian, F. (1961) 'The southern Italian peasant: world view and political behaviour', *Anthropological Quarterly* 34

Chomsky, N. (1978) *'Human Rights' and American Foreign Policy,* Nottingham: Spokesman Books

Chubb, J. (1982) *Patronage, Power and Poverty in Southern Italy: A Tale of Two Cities,* Cambridge: Cambridge University Press

Clark, I. (1988) *Waging War: A Philosophical Introduction,* Oxford: Clarendon Press

Clark, S. (1975) *Aristotle's Man: Speculations upon Aristotelian Anthropology,* Oxford: Clarendon Press

— (1982) *The Nature of the Beast: Are Animals Moral?,* Oxford: Oxford University Press

— (1985) 'Slaves and Citizens', *Philosophy* 60, 231

180   *Bibliography*

— (1989) *Civil Peace and Sacred Order*, Oxford: Clarendon Press
Clutterbuck, R. (ed.) (1986) *The Future of Political Violence: Destabilization, Disorder and Terrorism,* London: Macmillan
Coady, C. (1985) 'The morality of terrorism', *Philosophy* 60, 231
Confino, M. (ed.) (1974) *Daughter of a Revolutionary: Natalie Herzen and the Bakunin Nechayer Circle*, London: Alcove Press
Cox, A., Furlong, P. and Page, E. (1985) *Power in Capitalist Society: Theory, Cases and Explanations,* Brighton: Harvester
Crawford, J. (1988) 'Self-determination outside the colonial context' in Macartney
Crenshaw-Hutchinson, M. (1972) 'The concept of revolutionary terrorism', *Journal of Conflict Resolution* 16, 3
Crenshaw, M. (1986) 'The psychology of political terrorism', in Herman
Crotty, W., Kirkham, S. and Levy, G. (eds.) (1969) *Assassination and Political Violence,* vol. 8 of *A Report to the National Commission on the Causes and Prevention of Violence,* Washington DC: GPO
Crozier, M. (1966) *The Bureaucratic Phenomenon*, Chicago: University of Chicago Press
—(1973) *The Stalled Society*, New York: Viking Press
Dahl, R. (1970) *After the Revolution?*, New Haven and London: Yale University Press
Darby, J. (1983) 'The historical background' in *Northern Ireland*, Belfast and New York: Appletree Press and Syracuse University Press
Dicey, A. (1959) *An Introduction to the Study of the Law of the Constitution*, 10th edn, London: Macmillan
Di Palma, G. (1979) 'The available state: problems of reform', *West European Politics* 2, 3
Dogan, M. and Rose, R. (eds.) (1971) *European Politics: A Reader,* Boston: Little, Brown and Co
Donolo, C. (1980), 'Social change and transformation of the state in Italy' in Scase
Dornoy, M. (1984) *Politics in New Caledonia,* Sydney: Sydney University Press
Drake, R. (1984) 'The red and the black: terrorism in contemporary Italy', *International Political Science Review* 5, 3
Dunn, J. (1988) 'Rights and political conflict' in Gostin
Dworkin, R. (1968) 'On not prosecuting civil disobedience', *New York Review of Books* 10, 6 June; reprinted in Murphy 1971
— (1977) *Taking Rights Seriously*, London: Duckworth
— (1985) *A Matter of Principle*, Oxford: Oxford University Press

— (1988) 'Liberty is ill', *Index on Censorship*, 17, 8

Eekelaar, J. (1973) ' Principles of revolutionary legality' in Simpson

Engels, F. (1884) *Der Ursprung der Familie, des Privateigenthums und des Staats*, Zürich: Schweizerische Genossenschaftsbuchdruckerei (1902 *The Origin of the Family, Private Property and the State*, trans. E. Untermannn, Chicago: C. Kerr)

Farb, P. (1971) *Man's Rise to Civilisation*, London: Paladin

Farley, L. (1986) *Plebiscites and Sovereignty*, London: Westview Press

Farneti, P. (1985) *The Italian Party System*, London: Pinter

Feinberg, J. (1973) 'Duty and obligation in the nonideal world', *Journal of Philosophy* 70, 9

Finnis, J. (1973) 'Revolutions and continuity of law' in Simpson

Foot, M. (1978) *Resistance*, St Albans: Granada

Forbes, J. (1970) 'Do tribes have rights? The question of self-determination for small nations', *The Journal of Human Relations*, 18

Franklin, S. (1969) *The European Peasantry: The Final Phase*, London: Methuen

Freedman, L. (1983), ' Why does terrorism terrorize?', *Terrorism: an International Journal* 6, 3

French, S. and Gutman, A. (1974), 'The principle of national self-determination', in Held, Morgenbesser and Nagel

Friedlander, R. (1978) *Terrorism: Documents of International and Local Control,* New York: Oceana, vol. 1

—(1979) *Terrorism: Documents of International and Local Control,* New York: Oceana, vol. 2

—(1981) *Terrorism: Documents of International and Local Control,* New York: Oceana, vol. 3

— (1984) *Terrorism: Documents of International and Local Control,* New York: Oceana, vol. 4

Friedman, D. (1978) *The Machinery of Freedom*, New York: Arlington House

Galligan, D. (1988) 'Preserving public protest: the legal approach' in Gostin

Galtung, J. (1974), *Members of Two Worlds,* New York: Columbia University Press

Gauthier, D. (1977) 'The social contract as ideology', *Philosophy and Public Affairs* 6, 2

George, D. (1988) 'Distinguishing classical tyrannicide from modern terrorism', *The Review of Politics* 50, 3

Gerstein, R. (1984) 'Privacy and self-incrimination', in F. Schoeman (ed.) *Philosophical Dimensions of Privacy,* Cambridge: Cambridge University Press

Geurin, D. (1970) *Anarchism,* trans. N. Klopper, New York: Monthly Review Press

Gilbert, P. (1987) 'Just war: theory and application', *Journal of Applied Philosophy* 4, 2

— (1989) 'Terrorism: war or crime?', *Cogito,* 3

Gleason, J. (1980), 'Third world terrorism' in Alexander and Gleason

Goren, R. (1984) *The Soviet Union and Terrorism,* London: Allen and Unwin

Gostin, L. (ed.) (1988) *Civil Liberties in Conflict,* London: Routledge

Gottman, J. (1980) 'Confronting centre and periphery' in *Centre and Periphery: Spatial Variation in Politics,* London: Sage

Graham, G. (1985), 'Terrorists and freedom fighters', *Philosophy and Social Action* 11, 4

Gramsci, A. (1926) 'Alcuni temi della questione meridionale' in *La Costruzione del Partito Communista 1921–26: Opere di Antonio Gramsci,* 12, Turin: Einaudi

— (1971) *Selections from the Prison Notebooks of Antonio Gramsci,* ed. Q. Hoare and G. Smith, London: Lawrence and Wishart

Graziani, A. (1978) 'The Mezzogiorno in the Italian economy', *Cambridge Journal of Economics* 2

Graziano, L. (1978), 'Centre–periphery relations and the Italian crisis: the problem of clientelism' in Graziano, Katzenstein and Tarrow

Graziano, L., Katzenstein, P. and Tarrow, S. (eds.) (1978) *Territorial Politics in Industrial Nations,* New York: Praeger

Gross, F. (1969) 'Political violence and terror in nineteenth and twentieth century Russia and Eastern Europe' in Crotty, Kirkham and Levy

Grotius, H. (1913) *De jure Belli et Pacis,* edn of 1646, Washington: Carnegie

Guest, A. (ed.) (1961) *Oxford Essays in Jurisprudence,* Oxford University Press

Gutteridge, W. (ed.) (1986) *Contemporary Terrorism,* London: Mansell

Haksar, V. (1976a) 'Coercive proposals, Rawls and Gandhi', *Political Theory* 4, 1

— (1976b), 'Rawls and Gandhi on civil disobedience', *Inquiry* 19

Hall, R. (1971) *The Morality of Civil Disobedience,* New York and London: Harper and Row

Halliday, J. (1968) 'Structural reform in Italy: theory and practice', *New Left Review* 50

Hancock, R. (1975) 'Kant and Civil disobedience', *Idealistic Studies* 5, 2

Hare, R. (1967) 'The lawful government' in Laslett and Runciman

Harford, B. and Hopkins, S. (eds.) (1984) *Greenham Common: Women at the Wire*, London: Womens Press

Harington, Sir J. (1615) 'Of Treason' in *Epigrams both Pleasant and Serious*, London: J. Budge

Hayes, D. (1980) *Terrorists and Freedom Fighters*, London: Wayland Publishers

Häyry, H. and Häyry, M. (1989) 'Uraani halkeaa' ('Splitting the atom') in Malaska, Kantola and Kasanen

Häyry, H., Häyry, M. and Rossilahti, H. (forthcoming) 'Nuclear energy, value conflicts and the legitimacy of political decisions – the main lines of argument in a public debate in Finland 1986–7', *Rechtstheorie*

Hechter, M. (1975) *Internal Colonialism: The Celtic Fringe in British National Development*, Berkeley: University of California Press

Hegel, G. (1910) 'Absolute freedom and terror' in *The Phenomenology of Mind,* trans. J. Baillie, London: Swan Sonnenschein

Held, V., Morgenbesser, S. and Nagel, T. (eds.) (1974) *Philosophy, Morality and International Affairs*, Oxford: Oxford University Press

Herman, M. (ed.) (1986) *Political Psychology: Contemporary Issues and Problems*, San Francisco: Jossey-Bass

Heuston, R. (1961) 'Sovereignty' in Guest

Hobbes, T. (1962) *Leviathan*, London: Fontana

Honderich, T. (1980) *Violence for Equality*, Harmondsworth: Penguin

Horchem, H. (1987) 'Terrorism in Germany' in Stewart and Wilkinson

Hume, D. (1888) *A Treatise of Human Nature*, ed. L. Selby-Bigge, Oxford: Clarendon Press

— (1963), *Essays, Moral, Political and Literary*, Oxford: Oxford University Press

Ingold, T. (1974) 'On reindeers and men', *Man* 9

Iviansky, Z. (1986) 'Lechi's share in the struggle for Israel's liberation', in Tavin and Alexander

Jamieson, A. (1989) *The Heart Attacked: Terrorism and Conflict in the Italian State,* London: Marion Boyars

Jenkins, B. (1974) 'Terrorism works sometimes', Santa Monica, Calif: RAND

— (1980) 'The study of terrorism: definitional problems' in Alexander and Gleason

Jennings, I. (1959) *The Law and the Constitution,* 5th edn, London: University of London Press

Jennings, W. (1956) *The Approach to Self-Government,* Cambridge: Cambridge University Press

Jesudasan. I. (1984) *A Gandhian Theology of Liberation,* New York: Orbis Books

Johnson, J.T. (1975) *Ideology, Reason and the Limitation of War,* Princeton: University Press

Kant, I. (1922–3) *Werke,* ed. E. Cassirer, 11 vols., Berlin: Bruno Cassirer

— (1949) *Critique of Practical Reason and Other Writings in Moral Philosophy,* trans. L.W. Beck, Chicago: Chicago University Press

— (1970) (ed.) H. Reiss, trans. H. Nisbet *Kant's Political Writings,* Cambridge: Cambridge University Press

Kelsen, H. (1945) *General Theory of Law and State,* trans. A. Wedberg, New York: Russell and Russell

— (1966) *Principles of International Law,* 2nd edn, ed. R. Tucker, New York and London: Holt, Rinehart and Winston

Kipling, R. (1917), *A Diversity of Creatures,* London: Macmillan

Koch, A. (1943) *The Philosophy of Thomas Jefferson,* New York: Columbia University Press

— (1961) *Power, Morals and the Founding Fathers,* New York: Cornell University Press

Krimmerman, L. and Perry, L. (eds.) (1966) *Patterns of Anarchy,* New York: Doubleday

Kropotkin, P. (1976) *The Essential Kropotkin,* ed. E. Capouya and K. Tompkins, London: Macmillan

Kupperman, R. and Trent, D. (1979) *Terrorism: Threat, Reality, Response,* Stanford, Calif: Hoover Inst. Press

Lambeth (1988) *The Truth Shall Make You Free: The Lambeth Conference 1988,* London: Church House Publishing for the Anglican Consultative Council

Langgath, G. (1976) *Die Protestbewegung in der Bundesrepublik Deutschland 1968–76,* Cologne: Verlag Wissenschaft und Politik

— (1983) *Protestbewegung ... Die neue Linke seit 1968,* Cologne: Verlag Wissenschaft und Politik

Laqueur, W. (1987) *The Age of Terrorism,* London: Weidenfeld and Nicolson

Laslett, P. and Runciman, W. (eds.) (1967) *Philosophy, Politics and Society: Third Series,* Oxford: Basil Blackwell

Levi, F., Levra, U. and Trafaglia, N. (eds.) (1978) *Storia d'Italia – 2*, Florence: La Nuova Italia

Lieven, D. (1989) 'Gorbachev and the nationalities', *Conflict Study* 216, Institute for the Study of Conflict

Linkola, P. (1986), *Vihreän Liikkeen tavoiteohjelma (The Programme of the Green Movement)*, Järvenpää: Copycorner

Locke, J. (1956) *The Second Treatise of Government and A Letter Concerning Toleration*, ed. J. Gough, Oxford: Blackwell

Lodge, J. (ed.) (1981) *Terrorism: A Challenge to the State*, Oxford: Martin Robertson

— (1988) *The Threat of Terrorism*, Brighton: Wheatsheaf

Lutz, V. (1962) *Italy: A Study in Economic Development*, Oxford: Oxford University Press

Mabbott, J. (1947) *The State and the Citizen*, London: Hutchinson

Macartney. W. (ed.) (1988), *Self-Determination in the Commonwealth*, Aberdeen: Aberdeen University Press

Macfarlane, L. (1968) 'Justifying political disobedience', *Ethics* 79

MacFarlane, S. (1985) *Superpower Rivalry and Third World Radicalism: The Idea of National Liberation*, London: Croom Helm

McGurn, W. (1987) *Terrorist or Freedom Fighter? The Cost of Confusion*, London: Institute for European Defence and Strategic Studies

MacIntyre, A. (1981) *After Virtue*, London: Duckworth

Mackie, J. (1977) *Ethics: Inventing Right and Wrong*, Harmondsworth: Penguin Books

Magee, J. (1974) *Northern Ireland: Crises and Conflict*, London and Boston: Routledge & Kegan Paul

Malaska, P. and Kasanen, P. (1987) *Ydinvoima – kohtalon kysymys? (Nuclear Energy – The Ultimate Question?)*, with English abstract, Reports from the Finnish Ministry of Commerce and Industry, Energy Department, Series B, no. 63, Helsinki

Malaska, P., Kantola, I. and Kasanen, P. (eds.) (1989) *Energiapolitiikan arvoristiriidat (Values in Reasoning on Energy Policy)*, with English abstract, Publications of the Turku School of Economics, Series A-1, Turku

Martin, R. (1969) 'Civil disobedience', *Ethics* 80

Mazor, L. (1978) 'Disrespect for Law' in Pennock and Chapman

Mendus, S. (ed.) (1988) *Justifying Toleration*, Cambridge: Cambridge University Press

— (1989) *Toleration and The Limits of Liberalism*, London: Macmillan

Meny, Y. and Wright, V. (1985) 'General Introduction' in *Centre–Periphery*

Relations in Western Europe, London and Boston: George Allen and Unwin

Merleau-Ponty, M. (1969) *Humanism and Terror: an essay on the Communist problem*, trans. J. O'Neill, Boston: Beacon Press

Mill, J. (1978) *On Liberty*, Harmondsworth: Penguin

Miller, D. and Siedentop, L. (eds.) (1983) *The Nature of Political Theory*, Oxford: Clarendon Press

Mori, G. (1981) *Autonomismo Meridionale: Ideologia, Politica e Istituzioni*, Bologna: Mulino

Morreall, J. (1976) 'The justifiability of violent civil disobedience', *Canadian Journal of Philosophy* 6, 1

Muraskin, W. (1974) 'The moral basis of a backward sociologist: Edward Banfield, the Italians, and the Italian–Americans', *American Journal of Sociology* 79, 6

Murphy, J. (ed.) (1971) *Civil Disobedience and Violence*, California: Wadsworth

Nagel, T. (1987) 'Moral conflict and political legitimacy', *Philosophy and Public Affairs* 16, 3

Navari, C. (1981) 'The origins of the nation-state' in Tivey

Nedava, J. (1986) 'The IZL and its role in the liberation of Israel from the British rule', in Tavin and Alexander

Nielsen, K. and Shiner, R. (eds.) (1977) *New Essays in Contract Theory*, Guelph: Canadian Association for Publishing in Philosophy

Norman, R. (1986) 'Civil disobedience and nuclear protest: a reply to Dworkin', *Radical Philosophy* 44

Ostergaard, G. (1981) 'Resisting the nation-state' in Tivey

Paine, T. (1792) *The Rights of Man*, London: H. Symonds

Pateman, C. (1985) *The Problem of Political Obligation*, 2nd edn, Cambridge: Polity Press

Pennock, J. and Chapman, J. (eds.) (1978) *Anarchism*, Nomos vol. 19, New York: New York University Press

— (1983) *Liberal Democracy*, Nomos vol. 25, New York: New York University Press

Phillips, R. (1984) *War and Justice*, Norman, Oklahoma: University of Oklahoma Press

Philp, I (1987) *Freedom Fighters: From Monk to Mazumbo*, London: Akira Press

Pisano, V. (1985) *Terrorism in Italy: An Update Report 1983–85*, Report of the Subcommittee on Security and Terrorism, for the use of the Committee on the Judiciary, US Senate, Washington DC: GPO

Pizzorno, A. (1966) 'Amoral familism and historical marginality', *International Review of Community Development* 15–16

Plamenatz, J. (1960) *On Alien Rule and Self-Government*, London: Longmans

Polanyi, K. et al. (1957) *Trade and Market in the Early Empires*, New York: Free Press

Pollack, B. and Hunter, G. (1988) 'Dictatorship, democracy and terrorism in Spain', in Lodge

Primoratz, I. (1989) 'What isn't wrong with terrorism?', Paper presented to the annual conference of the Society for Applied Philosophy

Quinton, A. (1967) (ed.) *Political Philosophy*, Oxford: Oxford University Press

— (1973) *Utilitarian Ethics*, London: Macmillan

— (1978) *The Politics of Imperfection*, London: Faber

Rajaee, F. (1983) *Islamic Values and World View*, Lanham: University Press of America

Rand, A. (1967) *Capitalism: The Unknown Ideal*, New York: New American Library

Raphael, D. (1974) *Problems of Political Philosophy*, London: Macmillan

Rawls, J. (1969) 'The justification of civil disobedience', presented to American Political Association; reprinted in Bedau 1969

— (1971) 'Legal obligation and the duty of fair play' in Murphy

— (1972) *A Theory of Justice*, Oxford: Clarendon Press

Raz, J. (1979) *The Authority of Law*, Oxford: Clarendon Press

— (1986) *The Morality of Freedom*, Oxford: Clarendon Press

Regan, D. (1986) 'Law's halo', *Social Philosophy and Policy* 4, 1

Rothbard, M. (1982) *The Ethics of Liberty*, Atlantic Highlands: Humanities Press

Rousseau, J. (1968) *The Social Contract*, Harmondsworth: Penguin

Ruffilli, R. (1972) *La Questione Regionale Dall'Unificazione Alla Dittatura 1862–1942*, Milan: Giuffre

Runciman, W. (1963) *Social Science and Political Theory*, Cambridge: Cambridge University Press

Russell, B. (1961) 'Civil disobedience', *New Statesman*, 16 February

Sahlins, M. (1972) *Stone Age Economics*, London: Tavistock Press

Salmon, A. (1959) *La Terreur Noire: Chronique du Mouvement Libertaire*, Paris: Pauvet

Scase, R. (ed.) (1980) *The State in Western Europe*, Beckenham: Croom Helm

Schmid, A. (1988) *Political Terrorism*, 2nd edn, Amsterdam and New Brunswick: North-Holland Publishing and Transaction Books

Shils, E. (1961) 'Centre and periphery' in *The Logic of Personal Knowledge: Essays Presented to Michael Polanyi*, London: Routledge and Kegan Paul

Shonfield, A. (1965) *Modern Capitalism: The Changing Balance of Public and Private Power*, Oxford: Oxford University Press

Sidgwick, H. (1891) *The Elements of Politics*, London: Macmillan

Silverman, S. (1968) 'Agricultural organisation, social structure and values in Italy: amoral familism reconsidered', *American Anthropologist* 70

Simmons, J. (1979) *Moral Principles and Political Obligations*, Princeton: Princeton University Press.

Simpson A. (ed.) (1973) *Oxford Essays in Jurisprudence: Second Series*, London: Oxford University Press

Simpson, P. (1986) 'Just war theory and the IRA', *Journal of Applied Philosophy* 3, 1

Singer, P. (1973) *Democracy and Disobedience*, Oxford: Clarendon Press

Smart, B. (1978) 'Defining civil disobedience', *Inquiry* 21

Smith, M. (1973) 'Is there a *prima facie* obligation to obey the law?', *Yale Law Journal* 82, 5

Spencer, H. (1969) *The Man versus the State*, ed. D.G. Macrae, Harmondsworth: Penguin

Spooner, L. (1972) 'Letter to Grover Cleveland' (1886) in *Let's Abolish Government*, New York: Arno Press

Stewart, A. and Wilkinson, P. (eds.) (1987) *Contemporary Research on Terrorism*, Aberdeen: Aberdeen University Press

Sumner, L. (1977) 'Rawls and the contract theory of civil disobedience' in Nielsen and Shiner

Tarrow, S. (1967) *Peasant Communism in Southern Italy*, New Haven: Yale University Press

— (1977) *Between Centre and Periphery: Grassroots Politicians in Italy and France*, New Haven: Yale University Press

— *et al.* (1978) 'Introduction' in Graziano, Katzenstein and Tarrow

Tavin, E. and Alexander, Y. (eds.) (1986) *Terrorists or Freedom Fighters*, Fairfax, VA: Hero Books

Teichman, J. (1986) *Pacifism and the Just War*, Oxford: Blackwell

Thackrah, J. (1987a) 'Terrorism: a definitional problem' in Stewart and Wilkinson

Thackrah, J. (1987b) 'Freedom-fighters' in *Encyclopedia of Terrorism and Political Violence*, London: Routledge

Thornton, P. (1989) *Decade of Decline: Civil Liberties in the Thatcher Years*, London: National Council for Civil Liberties

Tivey, L. (ed.) (1981) *The Nation-State*, Oxford: Martin Robertson

Tönnies, F. (1971) *On Sociology: Pure, Applied and Empirical*, Chicago: University of Chicago Press

Tucker, D. (1980) *Marxism and Individualism*, Oxford: Blackwell

Tur, R.H.S. (1985) 'Paternalism and the Criminal Law', *Journal of Applied Philosophy* 2, 2

United Nations (1985) *The International Bill of Human Rights*, New York: United Nations

Voegelin, E. (1952) *The New Science of Politics*, Chicago: Chicago University Press

von Beyme, K. (ed.) (1988) *Right-wing Extremism in Western Europe*, London: Frank Cass

Waldron, J. (1988) 'Locke: toleration and the rationality of persecution', in Mendus 1988

Walicki, A. (1982) *Philosophy and Romantic Nationalism*, Oxford: Oxford University Press

Walzer, M. (1973) *Just and Unjust Wars*, New York: Basic Books

— (1983) *Spheres of Justice*, Oxford: Blackwell

Ward, C. (1973) *Anarchy in Action*, London: Allen and Unwin

Warner, M. (1989) *Philosophical Finesse: Studies in the Art of Rational Persuasion*, Oxford: Clarendon Press

Wasserstrom, R. (1961) 'Disobeying the law', *Journal of Philosophy* 58, 21

— (1980) *Philosophy and Social Issues: Five Studies*, Notre Dame, Indiana, and London: University of Notre Dame Press

Weber, M. (1946) *From Max Weber: essays in sociology*, eds. H.H. Gerth and C. Mills, New York: Oxford University Press

Weber, M. (1964) *The Theory of Economic and Social Organization*, ed. T. Parsons, Glencoe, Illinois: The Free Press

Whelan, F. (1983) 'Prologue: democratic theory and the boundary problem' in Pennock and Chapman

Wilkinson, P. (1974) *Political Terrorism*, London: Macmillan

— (1977; revised edn 1986) *Terrorism and the Liberal State*, London: Macmillan

— (1983) *The New Fascists*, London: Pan

— (1989) 'Ethical defences of terrorism: defending the indefensible', *Terrorism and Political Violence* 1, 1

Williams, B. (1973) 'Deciding to believe' in *Problems of the Self*, Cambridge: Cambridge University Press

Williams, H. (1983) *Kant's Political Philosophy*, Oxford: Blackwell

Wilson, T. (1989) *Ulster: Conflict and Consent*, Oxford: Blackwell

Wodehouse, P. (1953) *The Code of the Woosters*, Harmondsworth: Penguin

Woozley, A. (1976) 'Civil disobedience and punishment', *Ethics* 86

Zwiebach, B. (1975) *Civility and Disobedience*, Cambridge: Cambridge University Press

Index